Advance Praise for *Bey*

"Companies are facing new, tough questions from stakeholders about their sustainability performance. But how should organizations communicate what they're doing to employees, customers, investors, and more? And how do they do that without making embarrassing mistakes or greenwashing? *Beyond the Green Team* offers practical (and pithy) help on how to make the most of these critical moments of communication and connection."

—Andrew Winston, sustainability advisor and best-selling author of *Green to Gold* and *Net Positive*

"This is an idea whose time has come. I have searched for exactly this topic so many times, but couldn't find anything comprehensive and specific!"

—Vivian Melody, Director of Sustainability and Communications at the Community of the Transfiguration

"This decade sees businesses of all sizes waking up to the challenges of greening their activities and attitudes. Whether it's your first day in a sustainability role, or you're a thought leader in sustainability, there is much to learn in this great book. It's packed full of tips, facts, and thoughtful guidance. Moreover, it's the perfect book if you work in senior management and you are new to business sustainability thinking. No matter how far along the journey you are, you will be scribbling down notes on how to kickstart/revive initiatives and how to pull together a strategic company-wide approach."

—Paul Foulkes-Arellano, Founder, Circuthon Consulting

Praise for *Material Value*

"Meticulous editing and a succinct style . . . Exemplary for its balanced and reasonable viewpoint, the text deserves to be classified as a reference tool for countless professionals."

—*Publishers Weekly*, BookLife Prize

"An engrossing, comprehensive overview of sustainable manufacturing and recycling and the challenges to expanding their adoption."

—*Kirkus Reviews*

"This book is an antidote to a world too dominated by extreme opinions: it is a detailed, balanced, and fascinating account of how we can make the modern material world more sustainable."

—Mark Miodownik, author of *Stuff Matters* and *Liquid*

"A comprehensive, comprehensible guide to the impact of everyday materials like plastics and metals. If you want to take informed actions to support a better world, read this book."

—Anne Janzer, author of *Subscription Marketing* and *Writing to Be Understood*

"The clear explanations of the benefits and costs of so many types of modern materials, along with their current disposal methods, are valuable to anyone interested in moving our society toward a zero waste future."

—Jill Lightner, author of *Scraps, Peels and Stems*

"In this compelling and informative book, you will learn about everything from chemicals and plastics to manufacturing and recycling, as well as what you can do as both a consumer and citizen to make for a more sustainable material world, all explained in a simple, clear, engaging style."

—David Biello, author of *The Unnatural World*

Praise for *Rethink the Bins*

"This well-researched guide clears up the many myths and mysteries of what happens to the nearly eight pounds of trash we Americans create daily. Should be required reading in schools to help future generations embrace a circular economy."

—James Dillehay, author of *Start a Creative Recycling Side Hustle*

"If you're looking for a resource that demystifies what actually happens to the things we throw away, *Rethink the Bins* is for you! It's an easily digestible and interactive read. Goldstein's compelling writing style inspires hopefulness and action amid the often confusing task of reducing household waste."

—Moji Igun, Founder of Blue Daisi Consulting

"Finally, a book on waste reduction for realists! Julia demystifies compost and recycling, and her worksheets make this guide personal for you and your area."

—Summer Hanson, Co-owner of Eco Collective

"At a time when we're dumping mountains of food in landfills and filling the oceans with plastic trash, it's clear we need to change how we handle the problem of waste. *Rethink the Bins* is a great place to start: a clear, practical, and informative guide to the ways our waste systems work—and don't work. It's a valuable resource for anyone hoping to learn how to leave less trash behind."

—Susan Freinkel, author of *Plastic: A Toxic Love Story*

Beyond the Green Team

Beyond the Green Team

*Aligning Internal and External Communication
to Advance Corporate Sustainability*

Julia L F Goldstein, PhD

Bebo Press

Beyond the Green Team

Aligning Internal and External Communication
to Advance Corporate Sustainability

Copyright © 2022 by Julia L F Goldstein, PhD
First edition, Bebo Press, Bellevue, WA

The paperback edition of this book is printed on demand, eliminating the negative environmental impact of printing large quantities of books that might go unsold and contribute to waste. Organizations seeking discounts for bulk orders should contact the publisher.

Cover design: Michelle Fairbanks
Typesetting: Anna Botelho
Editing: Amy Reed and Nicky Lovick

ISBN: 978-0-9995956-7-1 (paperback)
ISBN: 978-0-9995956-6-4 (eBook)

Library of Congress Control Number: 2022914632

Table of Contents

Table of Contents

Introduction

I'm in a drab hotel conference room in San Jose, California, struggling to stay awake through yet another semiconductor industry summit. My head jerks back to vertical, and I look down at my notebook. I'm supposed to be taking notes for a column about the event in *Advanced Packaging Magazine*. Instead, I write, "This is the most boring presentation ever."

From my seat midway back from the podium, I can't even read the paragraphs in ten-point font and the highly detailed charts on the slides. Yep, it's another case of death by PowerPoint.

I suddenly realize that my dissatisfaction goes beyond the quality of this particular talk. They aren't all this bad. Many of the speakers do a fine job of engaging the audience. The problem is that I've decided I'm tired of writing about the technology behind gadgets.

It's not that the technology that goes into building circuits doesn't fascinate me. I just wish I could be involved in applications that benefit society. What about the renewable energy sector? I remember when I made a solar-powered marshmallow cooker in summer school when I was ten years old. That was fun!

This epiphany, if I can call it that—the realization that I want to do something that benefits society—happened in 2008, the first of many turning points in my sustainability journey. I thought about writing for the solar power industry, but that didn't work out. It would be another

1

decade before I wrote my first book. *Material Value*, which came out in 2019, is about how manufacturers can better understand and use materials like plastics and metals. In the introduction, I write, "This is the perfect time to publish a book looking at sustainability through a lens of materials extraction, processing, use, and disposal."

In retrospect, 2019 was, in some ways, a bit too early. Many businesses were not ready to take a critical look at the environmental impact of their manufacturing processes. Three years later, the business world is changing its tune after a global pandemic wreaked havoc on supply chains, and extreme weather crises have become all too common.

Business leaders are now actively looking for ways to make manufacturing more sustainable. In 2022, when I tell people that I work with manufacturing companies to help them advance their sustainability journeys, their ears perk up. More and more, I hear, "Yes, we need this."

Material Value talked a lot about sustainable manufacturing. It focused on how things are made and how they could be made in a better way.

This book is different. While the examples come from manufacturing sectors like semiconductors, aerospace, and consumer goods, the focus is communication. How you talk about sustainability within and beyond your walls affects your company's ability to redesign products and processes with environmental impact in mind. This book offers a framework for starting and deepening the conversations, including ways to get around common obstacles that can stall sustainability programs.

The reason I focus on manufacturing industries is twofold. First, that's where my experience lies—I'll get into that shortly. Second, I'm addressing manufacturers because that is where the greatest opportunity to improve sustainability lies. Individuals and service-based businesses can make a difference, but their reach is more limited. Unless we find a way to manufacture goods while severely restricting pollution and the use of fossil fuels, the small changes will not do enough.

I started my career in the semiconductor packaging industry. As a process development engineer, I worked with colleagues inside my company and with suppliers to choose materials that connect silicon computer chips to circuit boards and protect the chips from damage due to heat generation, moisture, or vibration. During my time as an engineer, I represented my company as part of a consortium of five companies developing technology standards. My participation in that project allowed me to collaborate with people who would otherwise be competitors. We recognized that our entire industry could advance by working together and sharing knowledge. Each member company maintained its unique approach to designing products and processes. Together, though, we had a greater influence on industry trends.

My path from engineer to writer came naturally. As an engineer, I gravitated toward writing quarterly reports for government contracts and articles for publication in trade journals.

In my two decades of experience as a writer, I've covered multiple manufacturing industries, including semiconductors, medical devices, printing, and transportation. I have worked as a journalist for trade publications, a market research analyst, and a content writer. I appreciate marketing professionals' enthusiasm for their companies and products. But I've also seen disconnects between many employees' concerns about social and environmental issues and the practices of their employers.

My business, JLFG Communications, has evolved since I founded it in 2011. I still help companies tell their stories through content like white papers and blog posts. My business now also offers workshops and corporate training about sustainable manufacturing and sustainability communications. My clients build awareness, gain knowledge, and broaden their perspectives through these programs.

My overall message is that actions matter, but so do words. How your company communicates to employees, customers, and investors says a lot about how the company approaches sustainability. More regular, more honest communication inside the company and to outside stakeholders will fuel a functional sustainability program that will be much more likely to meet its goals.

The benefits of better sustainability communication are enormous. What you say within and beyond your walls affects your ability to attract employees, customers, and investors. You can improve:

- Employee engagement, satisfaction, and retention
- Company reputation and customer loyalty
- Long-term financial gain

These benefits are what will draw in the skeptics and naysayers. When their financial future is on the line, they will pay attention. But it's not necessary to wait until all companies in all industries understand the need to move and to move fast.

I am writing to my primary audience—manufacturing industry professionals who care about people and the planet and want their workplace to reflect their values. You have a long-term perspective and also understand that we need action now.

I address much of my advice to sustainability directors, but you don't need that job title to benefit from this book. You might be in charge of sustainability, or perhaps you lead a marketing, design, R&D, or operations team. As you will see in Chapter 2, companies benefit when employees from all these departments participate in sustainability efforts. Individual contributors without official leadership titles can also be part of the solution. If you are early in your career, you likely bring a passion for sustainability that can make you a leader regardless of your job title and inspire your more senior colleagues.

If your company doesn't manufacture physical products, you might wonder if this book is for you. The messages here about communication and collaboration are relevant for nearly any company with at least one hundred employees. The examples are relatable to companies situated anywhere in a manufacturing supply chain. For example, Apple Computer doesn't make iPhones. They outsource manufacturing to suppliers.

Whether you have five or twenty-five years of experience in the business world, you can make a difference at your company. It all starts with honest communication, which is exactly what we will explore in depth in the following chapters.

How This Book is Organized

The five chapters in this book flow logically from one to the next. Chapter 1 sets the stage with an overview of sustainability trends, my take on sustainability, and why profit cannot be the only driving force behind business decisions. Change needs to start inside each organization. But change also starts within each individual. The Action Steps at the end of Chapter 1 encourage you to think about your personal sustainability journey, in addition to where your company stands.

Chapter 2 delves into internal communications and the importance of building strong connections with coworkers. The chapter discusses how executives and employees communicate about sustainability inside the company and offers ideas about how to engage workers from all departments.

Chapter 3 is about external communication, with a focus on the content that organizations create to share their message about sustainability. It starts by examining company taglines and then delves into creating website content that will inform your audience and avoid greenwashing.

Collaboration is the theme of Chapter 4. This chapter shares examples of what collaboration can look like and how it can advance sustainability. There is also advice for employees at companies that are less than supportive.

The final chapter ties everything together with a description of the Five Stages of Sustainability Communications and a framework that can lead companies through the stages. It leaves readers with ideas about what to do next to advance sustainability at their workplace.

Each chapter of this book concludes with action steps. For some of the chapters, these are more like discussion topics. Starting the discussion can lead to action.

I encourage you to complete these, or at least start answering the questions, before moving to the next chapter. I also realize that you might just be eager to turn the page and find out what's coming next. Or you might need to set the book down and work on something else.

I totally understand, and I've put all the action step content into a workbook so you can see it all in one place. You can download the workbook at jlfgoldstein.com/green-team.

This book is short enough to read in one day, but you might want to spread it out to give the ideas time to sink in. It is also something you can come back to for inspiration when you have had a challenging day at work. If you want to make your workplace more sustainable, I congratulate you. Keep reading for insights that will guide you toward the results you envision.

Chapter 1

The Current State of Sustainability

So, what exactly does sustainability mean? Let's take a look at a dictionary definition.

The definition of sustainability includes two somewhat opposing ideas. In one case, it is defined as the ability to be maintained at a certain rate or level. An example sentence on the Merriam-Webster website says, "The sustainability of economic growth." That sounds like a bit of a contradiction.

The other part of the definition, which may be what you think about when you hear the word sustainability, is avoiding the depletion of natural resources to maintain an ecological balance. For example, "The pursuit of global environmental sustainability."

Can both definitions coexist? Can we have sustainable growth? I believe that the answer depends on how we define growth. As Kate Raworth argues in her book *Doughnut Economics*, an economic model of continuous growth is unsustainable. When we consume natural resources faster than the Earth can replenish them, we will eventually run out of the necessities to sustain human life.

My take is that growth doesn't have to equal expansion into something larger. Humans stop growing in height in our teens or early twenties, but we are never too old to stop developing our skills and knowledge. I shared my story of starting JLFG Communications at age forty-five on the podcast "Fresh Blood: Killing it After 40." Similarly, businesses can grow by developing new, more environmentally sustainable products and processes while retiring the legacy ones.

Through this book, I want to give you the knowledge to help your company grow sustainably. You might find that means shrinking some revenue streams and growing others. Those are difficult decisions that can best be made after honest discussions among leaders throughout your company. The next step will be to explain those decisions to customers and investors. The exercises in the book will give you tools to communicate tough decisions honestly and, ideally, improve your company's reputation.

The definition of sustainability is worth discussing and figuring out. What does it mean for your organization to last for the long term without depleting natural resources? It's a big challenge. Unless you start the conversation, though, the default will be business as usual until that approach no longer works. At that point, it might be too late for your company to stay in business.

Responding to Pressures

Your company may be getting pressure from many directions to become more environmentally sustainable. Investors, governments, and customers are looking for action. They want to see big changes. Switching from disposable to reusable coffee cups in the company cafeteria is not going to cut it. If you are in an industry that is not yet feeling the pressure, are you going to wait until these pressures force your company to change, or will you start now?

Investors

Investors in many sectors are asking about how you're approaching environmental, social, and governance (ESG) practices. Demand for disclosing nonfinancial data that affects risk is growing.[1] Investors want to know about your greenhouse gas emissions, how much waste you are creating, and how you treat employees around the world. The need for ESG disclosure is especially relevant for public companies, but private investors also care about ESG issues.

Governments

Depending on where your facilities are based, local governments may be imposing new regulations. You may face hefty financial penalties if you are not in compliance. If your company operates in multiple locations, the requirements probably vary from place to place. Will you do the minimum required to comply with each set of local regulations or adjust policies company-wide to match the most stringent ones?

Customers

If your company makes consumer goods, your customers may be asking probing questions about your ingredients or packaging. They may demand that your facilities are safe for workers and the surrounding community.

Environmental impact is often a secondary consideration, but it is becoming a higher priority for many customers. Companies that offer products that meet customer demand for more sustainable solutions will thrive in the long term. Research commissioned by the World Wildlife Federation shows a dramatic increase in consumers searching for sustainable goods from 2016 to 2020.[2] The report based on that research quoted a survey where 50 percent of participants said they had switched brands to support products that protect the environment. Switching brands shows action, not merely intention. If you're reading this book, I imagine that you want your brands to be the ones consumers switch to instead of abandon.

Customers are asking about ethical sourcing of ingredients and pressuring brands to share data. Companies that make it easy for customers and other stakeholders to find the information they need and get their questions answered, will be seen as more trustworthy. That applies to more than just sustainability, of course. Customers first want to know how the product will help them solve a problem or accomplish something. They will only keep buying if the product works as advertised. Investors want to see a financial return. Governments want your company to be an asset to the community rather than a liability.

Do these pressures feel like a good thing, like a needed push to convince your company to make changes? Or do they feel like a huge headache and that taking on sustainability will cut into your profit margins? The answer depends in large part on your company culture.

Company cultures can shift toward sustainability. Walmart, for example, has made major strides in that direction. When I first saw Walmart featured in a positive light in articles on corporate sustainability and responsibility, I was surprised. Perhaps I shouldn't have been. The company website explains a fifteen-year timeline of sustainability initiatives ranging from powering its buildings with renewable energy to tightening supplier requirements. But original impressions are hard to overcome. I had long considered Walmart to be a company that prioritized low cost over everything else. But recent reports show that Walmart can be a good place to work, and the company gives back to local communities.[3]

The length of the journey to a place where sustainability is embedded in your company's culture depends on your starting point. Improved communication is one lever that will speed up the process. This book outlines steps that can smooth the path.

I realize that conversations about sustainability will not solve everything. Talk does not necessarily lead to action. Business is still driven by the need to make a profit, and financial pressures are real. But without honest, open communication, change will not happen.

Profit is Not the Only King

All the major equipment manufacturers have to show
their good financial performance to stockholders. So,
they mainly focus on how to maximize their profit level.

—Bruce Kim, CEO, SurplusGLOBAL

The mantra of "profit is king" and the desire to put shareholder value above all other priorities have defined capitalism for decades. But it doesn't have to be that way. In fact, it can't. Not only is the pursuit of profit at all costs unsustainable for the environment, but it is also unsustainable for business. Shareholders cannot continue to hold all the power.

More companies are considering what's called the triple bottom line—people, planet, profit—rather than making profit the only driving force. When companies commit to the triple bottom line, all three aspects must be in balance. They all influence any corporate decisions.

Fortunately, the emphasis is shifting. Green business proponents have been shouting from the rooftops for decades. For too long, many business leaders refused to listen. The tone has been changing, especially in the past two years.

The triple bottom line concept is not new. It dates back to 1994. But multiple global crises have made it clear that all businesses must embrace it for our society to continue long enough for the babies born in 2022 to live to old age. Embracing the triple bottom line in a beneficial way means shifting priorities. Ideally, companies can use the concept to commit to actions that improve the lives of their employees and customers, even if the short-term profit takes a hit.

The drive toward sustainability is relevant for all industries, but not all industries contribute to the problems—or the solutions—to the same degree. Yes, it is great when companies install solar panels on their office buildings or switch to energy-efficient lighting. But those changes can only take us so far. We need to change the way we make things.

The social and environmental impact of manufacturing industries is much greater than for service-based industries. Manufacturing, therefore, needs to step up and drive change. Manufacturing is a broad term that encompasses the following industries, and probably more that I haven't listed:

- ► Energy

- ► Transportation

- ► Machinery

- ► Consumer goods

- ► Medical equipment

▶ Computer hardware

▶ Chemicals

▶ Agriculture

The industries above cannot pursue a growth at all costs model. They must drastically reduce the amount of energy and resources they are consuming to make their products.

I published an article on Earth Day 2022 where I talk about Earth Overshoot Day.[4] That is the day when humanity has collectively consumed as much as the Earth can replenish in a year. In 1970, Earth Overshoot Day was on December 30. In 2022, it happened on July 28. The data is a bleak warning about the effects of unconstrained growth.

Data from the U.S. Environmental Protection Agency (EPA) divides this country's greenhouse gas emissions by sector. Transportation was responsible for 27 percent and industry—a category that covers several of the manufacturing industries listed above—accounted for 24 percent in 2020.[5]

Change needs to go beyond reductions on a per-product, per-kilogram, or per-revenue basis. Those reductions are helpful and can be a good place to start. The problem is that highlighting those successes can make it sound as though manufacturers have done enough. Reductions in greenhouse gas emissions must be absolute. From the viewpoint of climate change and pollution, consuming 30 percent less energy per widget produced does little good if the company makes twice as many widgets as it did the year before.

Change will be most effective if it starts at the design phase, and it must also involve employees throughout various departments, divisions, and locations. Chapter 2 says more about how employees in various roles can get involved in sustainability. Yes, companies can improve one product or one facility at a time if they don't have the resources to overhaul everything at once. But they need a plan to rethink all their products.

In some cases, companies that are heavily invested in certain industries may need to completely change their businesses and stop making harmful products. But all manufacturers can benefit from rethinking how and where they make, package, and deliver their products.

Many companies are starting to look a lot more critically at their supply chain. They are going beyond what's happening inside their buildings and factories. They are looking upstream to consider where they buy the materials, equipment, and supplies they need to run their business. And they are looking downstream at what happens to their products once they reach the customer.

What Sustainability Professionals are Saying

In my work as a consultant, I have interviewed dozens of employees in charge of sustainability at companies large and small. When I asked them what they wished for, they said they needed more resources. They wanted bigger budgets, more people helping advance their initiatives, greater knowledge about sustainability throughout their company, and better tools to evaluate their results.

I did not find it surprising that sustainability professionals wish for larger budgets. At companies where profit is the top priority, budget allocations tend to go to projects that can offer a rapid return on investment. Sustainability initiatives are not often seen that way. Employees get pressure to demonstrate that their programs will boost the company's bottom line. If they cannot do that, the funding doesn't come their way.

The lack of funding is an unfortunate consequence of short-term thinking. But there are ways to break through the barriers, and this book offers many suggestions.

Fortunately, not all sustainability programs require financial investments. Sometimes they involve a shift in mindset and priorities. Or expenses in one area can be offset in savings in another.

It can be lonely being the sole sustainability professional at a company. Without the support of colleagues, some people I interviewed felt frustrated and overwhelmed. As one sustainability professional told me, "I can't take on new projects because I also have an administrative role . . . I've not been trained in sustainability. So it's a bit too much right now."

Many people I interviewed have a sustainability board or council in place. They can collaborate with colleagues in charge of sustainability at other divisions in their company. They have good working relationships with their marketing team. But these advantages are not necessarily enough to foster as much interaction as they wish for. This is especially true in cases where the CEO does not appear to prioritize the efforts of the sustainability team.

I understand and sympathize with those who wish their colleagues were better informed. The drive to make a business more environmentally sustainable requires knowing where you stand so you can decide what to change. How can you reduce greenhouse gas emissions, hazardous waste, or water consumption if you don't know how much you are using now?

Gathering the data is a time-consuming job. It is not always easy to determine what data you need and how to calculate it. Fortunately, tools are available to streamline the process, but not all companies have access to the tools or the understanding to know which ones will work best.

Many people are also looking for better support from within their industry. That might be in the form of resources from industry associations. Actions from associations can demonstrate that environmental initiatives are a priority. They can offer training or connect like-minded members. When that doesn't happen, sustainability professionals can feel like no one appreciates their efforts.

A lack of industry support is challenging for people who are in charge of selecting materials or vendors. They wish there were a simple way to choose suppliers based on a sustainability ranking. Tools do exist, but not necessarily in a format that is easy to access and use.

Similarly, people want better partnerships within their supply chain. They would like to work with suppliers and customers to jointly tackle sustainability problems but cannot easily find a way to do so. The examples in Chapter 4 show that successful partnerships are possible.

Companies and industries vary in the maturity of their sustainability programs. I talked to people whose companies had been working on sustainability for decades. When they propose something new to improve ESG, nearly everyone at the company is enthusiastic. Employees list the company's sustainability as a key reason they want to work there.

I also interviewed people who were in the early stages of convincing their colleagues or their industry to make sustainability a priority. People just hadn't considered it and didn't know how to proceed.

One sustainability director I talked to struggles to build aware-ness among his customers. He expressed concern about the sustain-ability reports that customers have written using the Global Reporting Initiative (GRI) Standards. "There are clients who say they use GRI reporting. And when I speak to them, they don't have a clue what they actually reported." (Chapter 3 goes into more detail about the benefits and risks of sustainability reporting.)

Everyone I interviewed cares about sustainability and is familiar with the basics. They understand the urgency of reducing greenhouse gas emissions, pollution, and waste. They are working to address those issues.

But people's sense of agency depends on where they work. Those working at organizations where sustainability is embedded into the culture feel empowered and at least somewhat optimistic. Others feel that they are up against tremendous pressure. They are aware of the challenges their industry is facing but fear that their colleagues are not. Sustainability is not a top priority. Without support throughout the organization, some of the sustainability professionals I interviewed expressed frustration. They worry that they will not achieve the changes they envision. My hope is that this book can spur the necessary shifts that will give them and countless others like them, the support they need and deserve.

The Five Stages of Sustainability Communications

When it comes to communicating about sustainability, I group com-panies into five possible stages. I go into more detail about each stage in Chapter 5, but here is a brief overview.

Stage 1: *Unaware*—ESG and sustainability appear nowhere on the corporate agenda or in daily operations.

Stage 2: *Vaguely aware*—the company is beginning to realize that it needs to act.

Stage 3: *Aware*—employees realize that sustainability is relevant to their work, and the company website has a sustainability or ESG page.

Stage 4: *Involved*—employees are encouraged to prioritize sustainability, and external communication makes it clear that ESG issues are front and center.

Stage 5: *Fully engaged*—all stakeholders know where the company stands as an industry leader and are inspired to advance the sustainability agenda throughout the supply chain.

It is not easy to move from one stage to another, but our society needs all manufacturing companies to make the effort. When companies move from unaware to aware to engaged, they create more relevant and ambitious sustainability goals and are more likely to achieve them. This is true because employees throughout the organization are collaborating on solutions and working toward a common purpose.

The first steps are about building awareness. If people are not aware of the problem or what it has to do with them and their work, they cannot think of solutions.

Awareness is necessary and is also not enough. The hope is that awareness campaigns, when done in the right way, will inspire people toward collaboration and action. Everyone working together, whether in a small department, throughout a large company, or in an industry-wide effort, can do much more than individuals acting in isolation.

Industry associations can help, but only if the member companies are committed to action. When associations try to drive consumer awareness about sustainability, it takes constant effort to maintain momentum. As Scott Breen, VP of Sustainability at the Can Manufacturers Institute, states:

If you want to run a consumer awareness campaign to share your sustainability message, you should start with identifying the right consumer to target. This research on the front-end is critical so you can effectively break through the noise and resonate with your audience. Importantly, there should also be a commitment to a consistent and long-term communications campaign so you can go from building awareness and testing what works to get to the point of changing consumer behavior in a way that sticks.

Building awareness is something that takes time. Breen is talking about reaching customers, but companies first need to build awareness internally. That is the topic of Chapter 2. Companies that have taken that step need not wait until the outside world has heard their message to move toward stages 4 and 5. Once the employees are aware, they can become empowered to act. When systems are set up to make it easy for employees throughout the organization to help move sustainability forward, progress will happen.

What's Stopping Us

Saying that open communication is the key to advancing sustainability sounds simple. In reality, there is a lot more standing in our way. The key bottlenecks are cost, lack of knowledge, and apathy. Chapter 2 goes into these in more detail.

I have found that sustainability professionals overwhelmingly want support from their industries. Many wish that industry-wide coalitions would prioritize environmental initiatives. In some cases, this is happening. I share some examples in Chapter 4.

The need for industry-wide standards and expectations is especially relevant when changes make supplies or manufacturing more expensive. People feel that if their competitors had to comply with a set standard, then the entire industry could move forward. Otherwise, the leaders fear losing business to competitors who offer less expensive products.

Many are afraid to be the first to move. As one leader from an industry association told me, "The CEO says, I'll be the third person to do it, but the first two are going to bleed."

At the same time, businesses want to be recognized as responsible or best-in-class suppliers. When frameworks exist to rank suppliers on sustainability measures, those who excel can stand out. They can then win business even if they are not the least expensive option.

There is a need and a demand for better partnerships throughout the supply chain. People want an easier way to identify environmentally responsible suppliers. I hear the desire for both industry-specific and cross-industry collaboration. Both are possible.

Likewise, businesses and governments also have a complicated relationship. The specifics vary from country to country, but the big battle is working out how much government can or should regulate industry. Financial incentives, positive or negative, can encourage businesses to save energy or reduce pollution. But they can also encourage businesses to continue with policies that increase greenhouse gas emissions and cause irreparable harm.

Some of the people I interviewed said they wished for more regulation. The motivation is similar to that of industry-based standards. If the government forced lagging peers or suppliers to comply with more stringent requirements, that would level the playing field.

The companies that are ahead of the game, especially those that have long embraced sustainability as a key selling point for their products, tend to welcome regulation. That makes sense because they benefit by being already compliant while their peers struggle to catch up. Unfortunately, many businesses are not willing to change unless their hand is forced. When these are large corporations with substantial influence, they can argue that regulation stifles competition and convince governments to stand back.

This chapter has outlined the growing trend toward making sustainability a more integral part of doing business. We are far from a society where caring for people and the planet is a top priority for corporations. But every company that shifts its practices in the direction of sustainability makes progress toward that goal. The coming chapters offer advice for moving toward a more collaborative culture. To learn more about how you can improve things within your organization, read Chapter 2.

Action Steps

Below are several questions to ponder as you consider where you and your organization stand on sustainability. I encourage you to stop and write down your responses before moving on to the next chapter. You may download a fillable PDF workbook with these and all the end-of-chapter questions at *jlfgoldstein.com/green-team.*

1. **Your sustainability journey**

   When did you first become concerned about environmental sustainability? Perhaps it is something you have cared about since childhood. Or maybe your thinking evolved more recently. What specific events triggered a change in your position or opinion?

2. **The meaning of sustainability**

   What does sustainability mean to you? What do you think about both aspects of the definition from the beginning of the chapter? How is sustainability relevant in your life and to your work?

3. **Business pressures**

   Pressure can come from customers, employees, investors, governments, or financial institutions. Some pressures encourage you to move faster on sustainability, while others hold you back. What pressures is your company facing regarding sustainability?

4. **Sustainability communication**

   Actions matter, and so do words. How ready is your company to develop and deliver a believable, consistent sustainability message? If you aren't sure, the information in the following chapters will help clarify your next steps.

Chapter 2

Internal Communication— Connection

Many individuals working at manufacturing companies believe that it is vitally important to act on issues like climate change and social justice. But they don't necessarily connect those values to the work they do on the job. And employees are often not aware of where their employer stands.

When I gave a presentation on greening semiconductor manufacturing at an industry group luncheon in 2019, I highlighted companies like Intel that were leading the charge. One Intel employee came up to me afterward and said she had no idea that her employer was an industry leader in sustainability. Her job was to design electronic circuits for computer chips, and she hadn't looked beyond that to the bigger picture.

This engineer's experience is not unique. Employees who have been working in a specific role, sometimes for decades, are used to focusing on doing their job the best they can and earning their paycheck. If a company does not make a concerted effort to share its sustainability journey with employees and invite them to be part of it, it might not occur to them to ask. They don't always consider how their employer's products are helping or hurting people or the planet.

A CEO who I interviewed in 2021 admitted that he hasn't done a good job of communicating his company's role in promoting sustainability in the semiconductor equipment industry. "I think, first, we need to have a consensus internally," said Bruce Kim, CEO of SurplusGLOBAL, a company that refurbishes and sells secondhand equipment. "Actually, we are doing many, many things. But we are not organized in this, so many of our people don't know what we are doing for sustainability."

People need to know, and younger employees in particular are starting to ask. If a company wants to attract millennial and Gen Z workers, they need to be able to answer the question of how their company is treating employees, customers, and communities.

This chapter offers a framework for improving internal communication about sustainability. It starts with a close look at your company's claimed mission and vision. The next step is to build an internal sustainability team headed by the right leader, and then to move toward greater employee engagement throughout your organization. This chapter also addresses bottlenecks that can make this process difficult and suggests ways to break through them.

Mission, Vision, and Values

When examining how your company is talking about sustainability inside your walls, it's great to start by considering mission and vision. A company's mission and vision statements shows what it stands for, at least in theory. Mission and vision statements are a lens for examining a company's purpose.

It is often possible to tell from a company's mission statement whether sustainability is a top priority. For example, the mission statement might mention caring for the planet or supporting healthy communities.

For some companies, the purpose seems to be merely to sell as many products as possible to as many customers as possible regardless of the impact on people or the planet. Of course, the company's public voice doesn't directly say that. They don't say, "we don't care whether we are harming our employees or the local community." But sometimes it can be inferred. The mission is about excellence or bringing whatever the company sells into every household.

When a company says, yes, we do care, that is when we have to dig deeper. Are they just putting up inspiring posters on the wall or pretty words on their website? Or is there more to it?

The outward-facing message acts as a guidepost that offers insight about whether sustainability is a high priority. Messaging does matter.

The companies that win awards for being the best places to work don't win just because they offer free coffee or high salaries. The award-winning companies have a strong mission and vision at the core of everything they do. That sense of purpose motivates employees and inspires them. People aren't just coming to work to put in their time and get a paycheck. They feel that they are part of something bigger.

This is why it's good to start with what your company says it stands for. The official mission and vision statement, or the company tag line if you have one (see Chapter 3), offer clues.

Mission and vision statements are supposed to embody a company's purpose. That purpose should go beyond just making money for the shareholders. Ideally, the company should exist to do some good in the world through the products or services it sells.

Following are some examples of corporate mission statements.

Kao Corporation—"Kao creates high-value-added products that enrich the lives of consumers around the world."
This statement doesn't give a hint of the types of products the company makes. But perhaps that is the point. The statement allows for plenty of leeway to develop new product lines. So long as the products enrich people's lives, they could be additions to the portfolio.

Digging a bit deeper, Kao puts concrete goals behind its generic statement. By 2030, the company intends to ensure that "100 percent of our products will leave a full life cycle environmental footprint that science says our natural world can safely absorb." This more concrete goal supports the mission statement and makes it feel as though the company stands behind it.

Danone Corporation—"Bringing health through food to as many people as possible."
Danone's vision is more specifically focused on food, which is what the company makes. The vision can easily serve as a springboard to encourage leadership to develop concrete goals.

In 2021, Danone began calling itself a "société à mission," a purpose-driven company. Its nine-member Mission Committee is responsible for monitoring how the company's environmental and social values are being implemented. They are considering factors like health and nutrition, regenerative agriculture, employee engagement, and inclusivity.

In addition to mission statements, many companies promote core values. Brewer Science, a company that makes coatings and other materials for the electronics industry, says that its mission is, "Making a difference in the world through our people & technology." That is a nice but vague statement. What type of difference does Brewer Science intend to make?

The website shares a few more details with the company's list of six core values:

- Trust & Integrity
- Freedom with Accountability
- Win-Win & Mutual Respect
- Driven to Deliver
- Curiosity & Creativity
- Courage

Brewer Science has demonstrated its commitment to deliver on these values by becoming certified as a B Corporation. Certification requires companies to a achieve a qualifying score on the social and environmental performance assessment from B Lab, the organization that runs the B Corp process. (For more info on B Corps, see Chapter 4.) Brewer Science is the first in its industry to earn the certification, and hopefully more of its contemporaries will follow suit.

Aerospace manufacturer Airbus has also developed a list of six core values. These are:

- Customer Focus
- Integrity
- Respect
- Creativity
- Reliability
- Teamwork

The Airbus website includes more detail about how they incorporate each core value. The page includes videos featuring employees talking about the values. When I spoke to Airbus Culture Evolution Director Alice de Casanove, she gave me the sense that the approach is working. "The Airbus values are the foundation of our culture," Alice told me, "and it helps the employees to work together and make sure that we have a cohesion. We have a sense of belonging to something which is bigger than us."

Examining your employer's stated mission and vision is a useful exercise. If the company has been around for many decades, the original mission and vision statement from the founders may or may not still be in place. If it still exists, does it remain relevant? Or has its meaning changed?

Mission statements can endure. My alma mater, Harvey Mudd College, has kept the same mission since its founding in 1955:

"Harvey Mudd College seeks to educate engineers, scientists, and mathematicians well versed in all of these areas and in the humanities and the social sciences so that they may assume leadership in their fields with a clear understanding of the impact of their work on society."

This mission is perhaps even more relevant today, especially the part about understanding the impact of our work on society. That aspect was under-emphasized when I attended Harvey Mudd in the 1980s. Yes, I took courses in literature, history, philosophy, psychology, and music in addition to my engineering studies. But, for the most part, my peers and I didn't seriously consider the ethical and moral implications of our work as we started our careers. I don't fault Harvey Mudd. I received an excellent education and found amazing friends. The societal impact piece receiving less attention was merely a sign of the times.

Similarly, many companies that were founded over fifty years ago with a strong mission to improve the lives of their customers may have become sidetracked from that mission as the company grew because of societal pressure to prioritize profit over everything else.

Fortunately, societal pressure is now tilting toward environmental responsibility and social justice. Companies can revive long-standing mission statements or revise them to reflect where the business is today. Some businesses might find they need a complete overhaul.

In the action steps section at the end of this chapter, I encourage you to reflect on your company's mission, vision, and values. How do they relate to your day-to-day work? How do you and your colleagues embody or not embody the company's stated purpose?

Working with a Green Team

When sustainability is a high priority at a company, it becomes everyone's job to some degree. Still, there are usually a core group of employees in charge of directing and communicating the sustainability strategy.

Forming a Green Team

Companies sometimes create a "green team" to work on sustainability or corporate social responsibility (CSR) programs. Many younger employees are excited to be part of such a team. What they lack in experience, they make up for in enthusiasm. Millennials have heard the drumbeat of climate change warnings since at least their teens and have more to lose since they presumably have many decades of life and work ahead of them.

Senior employees with decades of experience may be eager to participate, especially if they are concerned about the world they are leaving to their children and grandchildren. But they may also be resistant to change at this stage of their career if they are near retirement.

Unless the Green Team has the power to make revolutionary changes in the organization, participants may quickly become disenchanted and discouraged.

Individual "green champions" or small, informal teams inside a company can achieve small wins. They might sponsor a day of service in the community or eliminate disposable coffee cups in the cafeteria. These actions can feel good and temporarily boost morale, but they won't lead to the kind of change that is sorely needed.

Support from the Top

For a company to make changes that truly advance sustainability, direction needs to come from the top and spread throughout the organization. It needs to encompass all departments, locations, and product lines. Bottom-up or grassroots initiatives have a hard time sustaining momentum if the management does not listen to or support their proposals. Enthusiasm starts high but fizzles out when suggestions get shut down. Employees hear the message that there is no time nor money available to focus on their pet projects.

Many organizations are recognizing this need for sustainability work to begin at the highest corporate level. Since 2019, dozens of companies have hired their first ever Chief Sustainability Officer (CSO). The CSO is in charge of overall sustainability strategy and is also usually responsible for ensuring that it gets communicated to every employee.

The sustainability leader doesn't have to hold the title of CSO. They might be called a Sustainability Director or might head up a different department like Environmental Health and Safety (EHS).

Sustainability Boards

Not all companies have a sustainability department headed by a CSO or similar leader. A Sustainability Board of Directors sometimes oversees sustainability strategy. This is separate from the Board of Directors that reports to shareholders, although that board should also be aware of and weigh in on sustainability strategy. Sustainability board members are usually employees.

Symrise AG, a producer of flavors and fragrances, has a nine-person Sustainability Board. Members include the CEO, CSO, head of investor relations, head of corporate communications, VP of HR, members of the corporate sustainability team, and sustainability leads for each major department. This structure supports a culture in which "sustainability is the business of all employees."[6]

Kao Group maintains an ESG Committee consisting of the CEO, other members of top management, and heads of business divisions. The Committee has the authority to make decisions on sustainability issues and implement programs. Kao also has an ESG External Advisory Board of industry experts from outside the company.

Forming a sustainability or ESG board or committee can be an early step in shifting corporate culture. The structure of the board can vary depending on the size and organizational structure of the company. Merely forming a suitable committee, however, is not enough. The committee needs to have enough power and responsibility. The top executives need to trust the committee and heed its advice.

The most effective sustainability boards involve top management. When the board includes or reports to the CEO, it is most likely to have real decision-making responsibility.

Toward More Effective Sustainability Committees

One mid-level manager told me that his company has a sustainability committee. At the same time, he was disappointed that the CEO didn't take sustainability seriously enough to fund this manager's wish list of programs. My sense is that a subset of employees, including the manager I interviewed, care deeply about sustainability and are frustrated about the roadblocks that keep them from achieving their goals. The company executives realize that sustainability is important for maintaining corporate reputation, but aren't investing as much as they could. As a result, change cannot happen at the required pace.

Regular communication from the sustainability committee conveys to employees that the entire company is on a path to change. The communication, however, should be two-way. If employees feel that their voices will be heard, they can share suggestions and request funding for projects. Every suggestion or funding request won't necessarily be approved or enacted. But if the lines of communication are open, employees will understand why the committee made the decision it did.

Companies do not need to have a formal sustainability or ESG committee to move forward with a sustainability agenda and communicate it to employees. Sometimes a policy that empowers all employees to contribute ideas can be effective.

For example, some companies announce big goals such as earning a zero waste to landfill certification or requiring that 100 percent of suppliers meet a particular environmental or social requirement. The management doesn't know up front how they will meet the goal, but they want to give it every chance to succeed. So they involve and empower employees. Brewer Science does something like this with its internal "waste watchers" program that celebrates reductions in ten categories of waste. It is based on Lean Manufacturing principles, and the company showcases examples of small changes that improve efficiency.

Building Your Team

Who is on the sustainability team for your company? Do you work with colleagues who have similar responsibilities as you do but for a different division or product line? Or is each division on its own to develop a sustainability strategy?

Working independently is not as efficient or effective as joining forces. The details may vary. Suppose your group is working to remove a toxic solvent from its manufacturing process. That problem sounds irrelevant to another group that doesn't use that solvent. But what if your group brings up the challenge in a company-wide meeting or online forum? Perhaps someone from that second group worked with a supplier a year earlier to solve a similar situation with their products. They can make the introduction. Putting your heads together can help the company as a whole improve its environmental performance.

The CSO or Sustainability Director and their direct reports are responsible for developing the company's sustainability agenda, but they alone do not implement it. To give the agenda the greatest chance of success, employees throughout the organization need to understand the goals and be empowered to participate.

There are benefits to including employees from all departments. Here are some reasons to include specific types of departments.

Marketing/Communications

The marketing and sustainability teams need to work together. As I say elsewhere in this book, collaboration between the people developing the strategy and the people communicating it to stakeholders inside and outside the company is essential. Marketing professionals can craft a convincing story even if they don't have all the information. But they shouldn't be left guessing about what to say.

Ideally the marketing team will understand the sustainability strategy and goals well enough to explain them to various audiences inside or outside the company. Strong connections between sustainability and marketing groups can smooth the way. Those connections build trust that empowers the marketers to ask the questions that will give them the knowledge they need.

Internal marketing communications can play a key role in getting employees from other departments excited about advancing the sustainability strategy. When it comes to external communications, well-informed marketers will be better equipped to create an honest message that neither oversells nor downplays achievements and intentions.

Engineering/R&D

For a company involved in designing and manufacturing products, engineers and technicians play a critical role. When technical personnel are not consulted, or when their warnings are ignored, things can go terribly wrong.

The National Society of Engineers' professional code of ethics requires engineers to "hold paramount the safety, health, and welfare of the public" when performing their duties. Companies should encourage their engineers to honestly disclose actions that might endanger workers or customers.

Some sustainability goals might only be met by revamping entire product lines. That requires involvement starting at the design and product development level.

Companies can also set aside R&D funding aimed specifically at meeting sustainability goals that are several years away. By communicating the goals with the R&D team—or, even better, getting their input when setting goals—research will be much more focused and likely to get results sooner.

Operations/Production

Employees involved in operations or production see what happens in the factory every day. These are the people who will take the sustainability strategy and put it into practice. They have valuable hands-on experience with the effect of changes in suppliers, policies, or regulations.

Operations teams will likely have practical ideas that will save energy or resources. They are often the first to observe leaks in equipment or inefficiencies in the production flow. If they are encouraged to fix the problems and share their experience with other groups, the whole company can improve.

Finance

Any new sustainability program you put in place must fit within a company's budget. A representative from the finance department can offer a reality check on what is affordable in what time frame. They may be able to shift funds between different departments or offer guidance on short-term costs versus long-term benefits.

The finance department also has insight into how the company is investing its reserves and may suggest changes that improve both ESG and financial health.

Human Resources

HR has an important role in communicating a company's culture and values. The HR department needs to be prepared to answer questions from prospective employees about the company's sustainability practices. The younger generations are more likely to want to know about a company's values before signing on.

An HR manager explained to me why she required her department to go into the office during the COVID-19 pandemic. Although many offices were shut down and millions of people were working from home worldwide, manufacturing did not stop. The HR manager decided that if the factory workers had to risk their safety to keep production running, HR was going to be there to support them.

HR may also get involved when writing or revising a company handbook. The handbook may explain the company's position on ESG issues and offer guidelines for expected behavior and reporting practices for any non-compliance.

In a company where all employees believe that improving sustainability is a high priority item and feel empowered to contribute, progress toward goals may happen naturally. But many companies are not yet there. They face bottlenecks that stop progress or make employees feel discouraged. In Chapter 1, I wrote that the three primary bottlenecks are cost, apathy, and lack of knowledge. The following sections of this chapter get into each of these issues in more detail. Another challenge, difficulty gaining customer buy-in, is related to all of the primary bottlenecks.

Bottleneck #1: Cost

Cost is probably the most common factor that stops companies from achieving their sustainability goals. I've heard from people who feel pressure to demonstrate that their sustainability initiatives will increase revenue. As one sustainability director told me, "If I were to take either one of those [materials in my product] and switch to a 100 percent bio-based material I would pretty much kill my profit."

That leader might think they don't have a choice. They feel that their hands are tied and they cannot change the materials in their product, so they might not even bring up the idea of bio-based materials with their colleagues or supervisor. The director has valid concerns, but perhaps there are options.

Assume that the director is correct that switching to bio-based materials but charging customers the same amount would drop the profit to exactly zero. What if they switched to bio-based materials but increased the price a small amount? Then the profit is non-zero. Could the company as a whole bear the reduced margins for this particular product?

Could the company substitute just one of the two materials? Would that help at all, or would customers be confused and not know how to dispose of the product?

What would happen if the company stopped producing the product? Would customers flock to a competitor that's making similar products from fossil fuels? Or is the company such a large supplier that their dropping out of the market would cause customers to panic?

What if the company gradually slowed production while ramping up production of bio-based alternatives at a higher price point? Would customers stay loyal and switch over to the more sustainable product?

What if the entire industry was comfortable with open communication? Could this company work with its competitors to gradually phase out the current product while committing to increased volumes of the bio-based version? They might together achieve the volumes needed to bring down the price of bio-based materials and make the product more affordable for customers.

Is switching to bio-based materials even the right option to consider? If this current product were not available on the market, what would customers choose instead?

These are all questions worth asking. Sometimes, however, fear stops people from asking them aloud. In an organization that encourages open, honest internal discussion, the director could bring up all of these what-if scenarios without worrying about retaliation. There may indeed be pushback. In a collaborative company culture, though, there is room to allow for pushback and keep working toward a solution.

Responding to Apathy

Bottlenecks like apathy and knowledge gaps can be related to cost, in that they affect the way employees respond to cost pressures. Breaking through them can pave the way to addressing the financial concerns.

Some people may find it hard to believe that anyone can be apathetic about sustainability in 2022. Don't we all understand the urgency by now? Yes and no. When the problems feel overwhelming or beyond our control, one reaction is to do nothing. Employees who have started projects only to have them shut down or set aside may feel uninspired.

Sometimes, employees feel that they lack agency and that their actions won't make a difference. If they feel like no one will listen or give constructive feedback, they tend to stay silent. If they have made an effort and nothing changed, they may become apathetic.

When the approval process for new initiatives is too cumbersome, employees will stop trying. It is human nature to want an easier way. People prefer a streamlined process that gets the job done.

Although more leaders are looking several years or even a decade into the future, public companies still need to demonstrate short-term results to shareholders. The problem is that new sustainability projects aren't always going to have anything to show this week or this quarter.

For example, building a company's reputation as a sustainable supplier takes time. It isn't going to result in a flood of new customers overnight. Existing customers might not prioritize sustainability. They see sustainable alternatives as more expensive—which may or may not be the case depending on the particular product—and are not looking at the bigger picture.

One way to overcome apathy is by committing to small changes before moving on to those that look overwhelming. If employees see signs of progress, that can be encouraging. When management also sends the message that every step matters and listens to suggestions to improve sustainability, that creates a more uplifting work environment.

Some changes are expensive and need to be phased in over time. Suggestions will be most likely to get approval if the people making them show that they understand the costs and are willing to be flexible. But a thorough analysis with accurate predictions of long-term savings or increased sales might convince reluctant executives to sign off on a faster timeline.

Lack of Knowledge

Another bottleneck is lack of knowledge. Employees haven't been trained in sustainability. They don't understand corporate data on greenhouse gas emissions, or they don't know how to estimate the impacts of their production processes. They don't know what to do with data from life cycle analyses (LCA), so the data just sits there and does no good. If companies have done these analyses and felt like they were a waste of time and resources, they are unlikely to continue doing them. Or perhaps they don't have the knowledge and resources to conduct LCAs in the first place.

With multiple ESG reporting frameworks out there, it can feel overwhelming to figure out which ones to use. Reporting is a big job, and it can seem unrewarding. Employees tasked with researching data or writing a report can wonder if anyone is even going to read it.

For companies that are starting from scratch with a sustainability program, it can be hard to know where to begin. Company-wide training about sustainability basics can help. Employees can enroll in online training courses, or you can bring in consultants to run full-day training programs or retreats.

There's also the problem of getting buy-in from employees who have been used to doing things a certain way for decades and don't want to change. If the existing ways are still allowing the company to stay in business and make its revenue goals, employees might not want to rock the boat. Why fix it if it isn't broken? The problem with that approach is that it might indeed be broken, but the cracks are not going to show up for years.

The tendency to keep going the same way you've always done things is common. But the most successful companies adjust with the times. Those that don't, find themselves irrelevant. For example, retailers need an online presence, ideally where customers can order directly from the website.

Businesses need to evolve, and one aspect of that evolution that is necessary now is to incorporate sustainability throughout the organization. Companies that haven't yet started the process can still do so. The time to start is today, and one way to start is with employees who are driven to keep what is working but overhaul what is no longer serving the business or society. It's time to empower the "green team" to go far beyond small, feel-good projects.

Buy-in from Customers

Customer buy-in can be another hurdle to overcome. In some industries, customers care about sustainability and are often vocal about their concerns. Manufacturers that make consumer goods—anything that individuals buy to consume at home—are seeing pressure from a segment of their audience to improve the sustainability of their products and their packaging. Many in this audience are willing to pay a premium for "greener" versions of the products they use every day.

Environmentally focused consumers are a growing segment. We have moved far beyond the days when they were considered a fringe market. It is getting harder for businesses to avoid meeting their needs. Demand for more sustainable packaging and shipping is growing. At some point, customers may stop buying from companies that over-package their products.

In other industries, customers are not prioritizing sustainability. Especially for business-to-business (B2B) products, customers just want a product that meets their performance requirements. Engineers sourcing components for their circuit boards are concerned about processing speed and other technical specifications. They might consider power consumption from the viewpoint of meeting battery life or heat generation requirements, but not necessarily because lower power is more environmentally friendly.

Businesses signing up with a recycling service might be doing it merely to comply with local laws. They are not necessarily willing to pay more for a service that ensures that everything they haul away gets processed in the most environmentally responsible way.

I spoke to an executive in the commercial recycling industry. He told me that he hears from prospective customers, "I love your recycling program, but I'm not going to put a penny toward it." Those customers expect that recycling should be free for manufacturers. This is a situation where government mandates that affect businesses can force things to change.

If customers are not demanding sustainability, it can be hard for a business to prioritize it. Doing so might risk customer loyalty in the short term. Looking out further than the current quarter or even a year or two, however, will paint a different picture. Fortunately, more and more companies are beginning to see that.

In the action steps section at the end of the chapter, I invite you to identify the bottlenecks that are present at your company. Meanwhile, let's look at some ways to improve communication and break through the bottlenecks.

Encouraging Communication

There are many ways that companies can communicate with employees and encourage (or discourage) two-way communication. These approaches apply to all aspects of business, but a company that excels will incorporate communication about sustainability into its overall communication strategy.

The following sections explain some popular communication channels that you can use to encourage better employee engagement.

Newsletters

Company newsletters are a common way to keep employees informed. But unless the newsletters are easy to access and offer content people want to read, they aren't much use. The information should be relevant, highlighting positive company news that goes beyond financial results.

If the newsletter talks about where individual employees or departments are excelling, people will be more engaged than if it looks like a bland corporate update. There is also an opportunity to remind employees about new policies. Are you working with a partner to reuse a waste stream from one of your factories? Make sure that everyone, even employees whose jobs have nothing to do with that particular waste stream, knows about the new opportunity and how it benefits all parties.

If done well, newsletters can boost morale and encourage employee engagement. If not, they can feel like (and be) a waste of time.

Newsletters don't have to be in written format. Airbus runs an internal company podcast. The first season talked about the employee resource groups and how people can participate. In the second season, they interviewed employees about what Airbus values mean to them.

Innovation Challenges

Businesses can run innovation challenges where employees offer suggestions to solve a problem the company is facing. These can be oriented around sustainability. For example, getting input on ways to meet a greenhouse gas emission reduction target or achieve zero waste to landfill.

Ideas may come from unexpected places. Yes, the R&D department probably makes innovation a priority. But suggestions to improve efficiency could come from anywhere. An open call for ideas is a great way to encourage everyone to contribute and feel like there is a way for them to be heard.

Fuji Oil Holdings, which makes plant-based food ingredients based on vegetable oils and fats, wrote about a recent innovation challenge in their 2020 sustainability report. An open call for employees' ideas on how Fuji Oil can contribute to the United Nations Sustainable Development Goals (UN SDGs) received 218 submissions.

The CEO and the Chief ESG Officer reviewed all the submissions and selected ten to implement. This is an excellent example of leadership. When the top executives take the time to listen to everyone's contributions, it sends a message that employees matter and that the company prioritizes sustainability.

Town Hall Meetings

I usually associate town hall meetings with politicians, but they can be a great addition to a business. It is a chance for the heads of divisions, departments, or the entire company to give an update and then open the floor for questions.

In a political town hall, the most effective meetings are those where the candidates go beyond their practiced sound bites to honestly answer questions.

The same is true for the corporate setting. If people feel that the CEO will merely repeat the same standard corporate spin, they will not be excited to attend a town hall.

When employees get honest, thoughtful answers to their questions, they feel heard. As a result, they are most likely to keep attending the meetings and keep asking questions.

"I don't know" is sometimes an honest answer. It is great to follow up with a promise to look into the issue or schedule a separate conversation. The next critical step is to fulfill that promise. When executives keep their word, that builds trust.

Posters and Displays

Visual displays in the workplace can serve multiple functions. Clear signs on trash and recycling bins tells everyone what to toss where. Prominent safety messages remind employees to follow proper procedures.

Statements about the company's core values can serve as a reminder about the "why" behind the work. This only works if the company espouses the claimed values. They have to walk the talk. Otherwise, the posters boasting about integrity or respect look like false promises.

Displays showing awards or certifications the company has earned can inspire continued efforts to keep up the good work. These displays show pride in accomplishment and reflect the sense that the awards are worth celebrating. They should be kept up to date. If the most recent award was from ten years ago, that is not a good sign.

Bulletin boards are also a place to post company news or important deadlines. Even if your company writes excellent newsletters, not everyone reads them. Putting information in multiple places increases the likelihood of it reaching employees throughout the organization.

For organizations with remote employees who work from home or from satellite offices, displays can be in the form of features on the website that highlight awards and news. Company blogs, which I discuss in Chapter 3, can feature employees and share stories that are of interest to them as well as to customers.

Employee Training

Training can involve onboarding of new employees, continuing education for those taking on new roles, and skill development for employees at any level. It can be done entirely in-house, such as a department head instructing all their direct reports on new processes or technology, or through an online course on cyber security that all employees need to complete once a year.

Many companies bring in external trainers or consultants. Others give each employee a budget they can use to pay for continuing education. This training can be about any topic that is relevant to employee development. One such topic is, of course, sustainability. I mentioned basic sustainability training in the section on bottlenecks.

Employees, including those with "sustainability" in their job title, are not necessarily trained in sustainability. If they don't understand the terminology or the strategy, they are not in the best position to implement it. Employee training is, therefore, an important piece of engagement for sustainability.

Kao Group conducts employee training on a variety of environmental topics including decarbonization, zero waste, raw materials sourcing, and life cycle assessments. That training is an important piece of the company's three-pronged approach to employee engagement: inform, inspire, and empower.

This chapter has covered several aspects of internal communications that can help build connections among colleagues. This internal connection and communication is essential for building and implementing sustainability goals. Unless a company is committed to honest, open internal communication, the external communication is likely to be inconsistent, confusing, or even misleading.

Once you've improved communication inside your walls, you will be in a position to share your message externally, make a difference throughout your industry, and extend your reach up and down the supply chain. The next two chapters offer advice and examples on how to do that.

Action Steps

Below are a series of six action steps to take to help you turn the information in this chapter into action in your company. You can download the workbook at jlfgoldstein.com/green-team to type your thoughts into a fillable PDF.

1. Reflect on your company's stated mission, vision, and values.

Consider whether the mission and vision ring true. If so, you are in a great starting place. If not, it may be time to determine whether a change in either the mission statement or your company's strategy is warranted. What can you do to encourage a more purpose-driven culture at work?

I encourage you to examine the mission and vision with a sustainability lens. Can you see your sustainability strategy reflected in the mission statement? Does your company's slogan or tag line reflect a slant toward sustainability? If so, great. If not, some changes may be needed.

2. Examine your sustainability team.

Who is leading the team, and who is a participant? Consider who else at your company could or should be involved as key players to develop and implement your sustainability strategy.

If you don't already have a sustainability board or other official group, you may want to form one. There are also opportunities to involve all employees in your sustainability strategy.

3. Identify the bottlenecks.

If your company is not moving as fast as you wish it would, what is stopping you? By identifying bottlenecks such as cost, lack of knowledge, or apathy from employees or customers, you can be in a position to break through. An employee survey can be one tool to help with the process.

4. Do a reality check.

This is where you evaluate your company's operations, including all product lines and locations. Then you compare that reality to the story the company is telling employees. Look for coherence or mismatch between words and actions. Identify the gaps or places where there is cognitive dissonance and talk about them openly. This is a hard discussion that will first need to happen in a small group where there is mutual trust.

5. Make a plan.

How do you want to communicate about sustainability with your employees? If the previous steps exposed large gaps, this will need to be done carefully to build or rebuild trust. If, on the other hand, you mainly saw a reasonable alignment between what you say and what you do, the process will be much faster and easier.

6. Evaluate and maintain your plan.

It is not enough to create a communication plan. Communication channels do not make honest communication flow automatically. Feedback will tell you whether the communication plan is working.

Do employees pay attention to posted policies and change their behavior? How many employees attend training sessions or meetings? Do they feel the programs are worthwhile or a waste of their time?

Once you evaluate the results of your communication strategy, you can keep what's effective and change what isn't working. The world and your industry will continue to evolve. It's important to revisit your plan regularly and decide if it still meets your company's needs.

Chapter 3

External Communication—Content

External communication about sustainability encompasses all the information that reaches stakeholders other than the employees. The information can be in the form of written content, video content, and online or in-person presentations. The stakeholders include customers, investors, financial institutions, nongovernment organizations (NGOs), and governments. The tone and content of external messaging says a lot about the company's purpose and values.

Much of the information in this chapter is based on insights I have gleaned from evaluating company websites. That is the place where an organization has the greatest control over how it positions its approach to sustainability and what content it shares with the world.

What's in a Tag Line?

Tag lines are often part of the public face of a company, especially for businesses that are selling consumer products. Customers remember tag lines. And sometimes tag lines are prospective customers' first impressions of a brand or a company. Many companies are known for their catchy tag lines that have become associated with their brand.

You probably know Nike's tag line: Just Do It. That's a tag line that inspires action. The message is to do the thing that you're considering.

Put on those running shoes, outfit yourself in that Nike-branded attire, and get out and move.

Other company tag lines are positioned as promises. These slogans are designed to make customers feel good about buying products or services from the company. But what is behind the promise? Here are a few examples to contemplate.

Danone—One Planet. One Health.

I find this one a bit odd. Of course we have one planet. The implication is supposedly that we must protect it. But one health? Danone is a food company, so they may be getting at the idea that we all have one body and it's important to fuel ourselves with healthy food.

Not everything that Danone makes, however, is inherently healthy. I would argue that yogurts with added sugar and artificial colors are not the healthiest choice. In Danone's defense, the company recognizes the disconnect and is reconsidering the health promise of its brands. Danone's Mission Committee, which I mentioned in Chapter 2, is working on that.

Umicore—Materials for a better life

This sounds like a nice promise, but it's a bit vague. Umicore makes catalysts that help vehicles run more cleanly and meet emission standards. But electric vehicles, which don't need emission controls, are slowly replacing gasoline-powered engines, making Umicore's catalysts irrelevant. Umicore does recycle various metals. More extensive recycling that can reduce the need to mine more metals is a step forward.

Do the employees at Umicore see their work as promising them a better life? Or do they see themselves contributing to a better life for Umicore's customers? I don't know the answer.

HP, Inc.—Technology that makes life better for everyone, everywhere
HP explains that this is a vision they strive toward. This promise seems overly optimistic. My HP printer is useful, but it isn't much of a factor in my overall quality of life. Even if more technology doesn't make life better in a big way, though, the company does some things right.

I interviewed HP Senior Director of Social and Environmental Responsibility Judy Glazer for my book *Material Value*. She told me that she sees sustainability as a natural extension to HP's long-standing focus on global citizenship, and she sees her role as moving the company toward its vision.

Philip Morris International—Delivering a smoke-free future
This is a relatively new tag line for this company that makes most of its revenue from tobacco products. The tag line, which is featured prominently on the company's website, makes it sound as though Philip Morris intends to stop selling tobacco products.

A closer look through the Philip Morris website reveals a different story. The actual plan is to shift toward tobacco products that don't burn but heat at lower temperatures. The message is: it's better to quit but we know that millions of smokers won't, so we want to offer an alternative.

It might surprise people that Philip Morris is among the ten companies that received a grade of A in 2020 from CDP on climate change, forests, and water security. CDP is an international nonprofit organization that runs a disclosure system that rates companies, cities, and geographical regions on their environmental impact.[7] A is the top grade in the system. HP also made that list.

DuPont—*The miracles of science*

This tag line replaced the oft-quoted and sometimes satirized "Better living through chemistry" tag line that the company used from 1935 to 1982. It reads as fuzzier and less prone to becoming satire.

Understanding science and using it to benefit society, however, are two very different things. And DuPont executives have often ignored the science when studies pointed out the health hazards of some of its products. The book *Exposure* by Rob Bilott tells the detailed story of DuPont's attempts to avoid responsibility for poisoning people with the perfluorochemicals (so-called "forever chemicals") used to make Teflon.

UPM-Kymmene Corporation—*Beyond Fossils*

UPM is capitalizing on the need to move away from fossil fuels to reduce greenhouse gas emissions. The company offers products in multiple business lines: pulp, timber, biofuels, energy, paper, plywood, biocomposites, biochemicals, biomedicals, forest, and raflatic (paper labels). Many of these rely on wood as the raw material, and in some cases the company's products offer an alternative to plastics sourced from fossil fuels.

The tag line seems relevant, but I don't know how much it inspires employees or customers.

Monsanto—*Growing Better Together*

Monsanto relates this tag line to the goal of feeding more people using fewer natural resources. It's a worthy goal. The company claims to promote the United Nations' Sustainable Development Goals for water use, climate action, poverty, and hunger.

But Monsanto is frequently maligned as an example of what is wrong with large-scale, commercial agriculture: overuse of pesticides, lack of crop diversity, and development of genetically modified organisms (GMOs). There are better ways of feeding the world.

Regardless of the tag line, Monsanto is hardly associated with a commitment to environmental sustainability and human health.

Tag lines are designed to draw attention. They can be inspiring. Unfortunately, as many of these examples show, they can also be misleading.

Just as internal communication should be clear and honest, so should all external messaging. Complete transparency in corporate communications seems like a nearly impossible ideal. The phrase "transparent corporate communications" sounds like an oxymoron to anyone accustomed to the idea that corporations share carefully crafted messages designed to highlight only the upside.

The Greenwashing Problem

You have probably heard the term greenwashing. It's the practice of making false claims about sustainability. The claims themselves may have some truth to them, but they are often made out of context or without telling the whole story.

One dictionary definition describes the verb greenwash as, "To express environmentalist concerns especially as a cover for products, policies, or activities."

Companies that lead with external communication about sustainability before honestly assessing their internal practices are at a higher risk of greenwashing. The marketing department might jump on the latest trends without really considering everything the company is doing.

In some cases, marketing messages deliberately mislead consumers and customers. Other times, marketers cling to evidence showing the company is moving in the right direction and highlight it. They don't stop to consider whether the story is the whole truth.

Marketing is not evil. Far from it. I work with marketing people all the time, and I love their passion for their work. I've taken on marketing roles myself. It's just that marketing, especially when talking about sustainability, needs to be done carefully. Consumers are becoming more wary. They're listening to what you say and what you do. Mismatches lead to distrust that erodes customer loyalty.

How much of a problem is greenwashing? That depends on the industry. It's especially a challenge for industries where the bulk of their revenue comes from fossil fuel extraction and consumption or where their manufacturing process is inherently resource-intensive or toxic.

It is no accident that the first industries that the Global Reporting Initiative (GRI) chose when creating sector-specific reporting standards in 2021 and 2022 are those with the highest impact.[8] They are, in order:

- ► Oil and Gas
- ► Coal
- ► Agriculture, Aquaculture, and Fishing
- ► Mining

Companies in these industries are evolving, but not necessarily fast enough. Giants in the oil and gas industry tout their investments in renewable energy and their goals for greenhouse gas emissions reductions while continuing to extract fossil fuels and even expanding those operations.

Anyone reading the fine print hidden in 100-page corporate reports can learn the whole story. But the public is not going to read the details. Even most customers will not take the time to read a sustainability report cover to cover.

Clean Creatives, a group of public relations professionals that have agreed not to work with fossil fuel companies, give an example. "Shell has even gone so far as to disclose to investors that 'as of February 11, 2021, Shell's operating plans and budgets do not reflect Shell's Net-Zero Emissions target,' even while widely advertising that target to the public and regulators."[9]

This type of advertising is greenwashing. It is deliberate and misleading. In reality, the fossil fuel industry is in a tough place. It is understandable that they want to tell people that they intend to change their ways. It is understandable that they want to share stories of lofty goals.

Unfortunately, however, the stories that they want to tell do not reflect what is really going on inside the companies. They have made public statements to appease stakeholders. But the actions do not match the words.

Greenwashing is in no way limited to extractive industries. It is prevalent in companies that sell fashion, food and beverage, and household goods. They tout recycled content in their products or packaging as though that is the solution that magically makes their industry environmentally responsible. One example is polyester clothing made from recycled water bottles. There are environmental advantages to using recycled instead of virgin sources, but it is still plastic and will shed microplastics when laundered. Also, many clothing companies promote overconsumption when they release new styles and patterns every season.

Many industries face public perception that their products are endangering human health and the environment. In some cases, this is true, but millions of customers still rely on the products they produce. It would not be responsible to suddenly pull entire product categories off the market without an available alternative. Not only would customers be upset, but millions of employees would lose their jobs.

In other cases, the public image simplifies things or makes blanket statements that don't tell the entire story. It is up to companies in the industry to set things straight, but that is not easy. The whole story often involves technical, scientific, or industry-specific knowledge that is beyond the grasp of non-experts.

The trick is to explain things in ways that customers, investors, or the general public can understand without hiding behind a glossy, carefully tailored image. Doing so can build trust. To build trust further, open the door and make the technical details available to independent experts who can verify that the public statements are valid. If your products or facilities have been certified by reputable organizations, sharing reports about those certifications is one path. If you claim to meet recognized standards, make sure you can back those claims up with data.

There's a fine line between wanting to promote your company's successes in greening your products or processes and overselling the progress you've made. Chapter 4 shows how some companies have struck a balance. They announce their sustainability goals and take pride in progress toward them while recognizing that there is still room for improvement and that their advances are not a complete solution.

Greening Your Website

"I realize how important it is for interested stakeholders
to go look at our site and see what we are doing on ESG."

—Jennifer Yuen, ASE Senior Director of
Corporate Marketing Communications

External stakeholders can access information about your company in various ways. One of the key channels, though, is the company website. It is the online face of the company. If website visitors cannot quickly find what they are looking for, they will move on.

Any company that wants to position itself as a leader, or even a participant, in sustainability will have a statement on the home page that makes it clear that the company considers sustainability to be important. The mission statements mentioned in Chapter 2 are good examples.

Before you revamp your website to make your company look like a sustainability leader, though, you need to *be* a sustainability leader. Otherwise, all you're doing is greenwashing. You should do the hard work of working through your internal communication before you task the marketing team with improving the external piece. As mentioned in Chapter 2, if you don't build strong connections between sustainability and marketing, the external marketing group might not tell the best story to inspire confidence and loyalty from customers.

If you've connected your company's mission and vision to sustainability, built your internal team, and engaged employees throughout the organization, it is time to revisit your website.

This is one place where collaboration between the sustainability and marketing teams is essential. As many of the examples in Chapter 4 show, companies that are leading the way in sustainability benefit from a strong connection between sustainability and marketing.

When updating content, you may also want to make changes to the design. Design updates can range from choosing a different font or colors—usually in the context of a brand refresh—to revising the page layout or restructuring the entire site. Website design, however, is beyond the scope of this book.

Regarding content, there are many parts of the website to consider. Relevant pages include Home, About, News or Media, Sustainability or ESG (Environmental, Social, and Governance), Blog, and Resources.

The table at the end of this section shows some of the pages that appear in the main menu of companies that earned top scores from CDP on climate change, forests, and water security in 2020. All of these companies have a page related to sustainability, and all but one includes a prominent link to that page. In some cases, they call it by another name.

HP is somewhat of an exception. HP's home page is more focused on product information, but its "About Us" section at the bottom of the page includes a sub-category of "Sustainable impact."

For many companies in business-to-consumer (B2C) markets, the consumer-facing website will be more focused on a catalog of products and how to buy them. Unless the environmental benefits of the products are key to the company's position in the market, information about sustainability is more likely to reside deeper within the website. Some B2C companies host a separate website aimed at investors or suppliers.

Whether you serve a business-to-business (B2B) or a B2C market, if you are on a mission to elevate the sustainability of your company and its products, that message needs to be heard.

Examples of Primary Navigation Website Pages

(Those in bold are where companies share sustainability information.)

Company	Sample Navigation Headings			
Fuji Oil Holdings	About Us	Investor Relations	**Sustainability**	News Releases
L'Oréal	Group	**Commitments**	Brands	Beauty Science & Technology
Danone	About Us	Brands	**Impact**	Stories
Kao	About the Kao Group	Our Brands	Research & Development	**Sustainability**
Firmenich	Facts & Figures	Our Legacy	Working at Firmenich	**Sustainability**
Mondi	About Mondi	Products & Solutions	Governance	**Sustainability**
Philip Morris International	Our Transformation	Our Science	Smoke-free Life	**Sustainability**
HP, Inc.	Explore	Shop	Support	**Sustainable Impact***
Symrise AG	Our Company	Newsroom	Investors	**Sustainability**
UPM	Businesses	**Responsibility**	News & Stories	About Us

* Not a primary navigation heading. The page appears as a sub-category of the About Us page, reached from links in the home page footer.

Home Page

The home page is the first place your prospective customers will see. There's an opportunity to say something about your company's position on sustainability so that every website visitor will notice it.

Consider the home page of Fuji Oil Holdings Inc., a company that makes plant-based food ingredients including many based on vegetable oils. It features a carousel with photos of food and plants. The captions include links to the company's Integrated report (a combination of ESG and financial reporting), a special report on Responsible Palm Oil, and a video called "Toward a sustainable food future."

Danone's home page includes a carousel that defines the company's commitments to human health and the environment, along with examples of how the company's products address the needs it claims to address.

One challenge is not to oversell the environmental benefits of a particular segment of your company's products or operations. Unless you consider the sustainability advantages in context, it is too easy to tell a story that's not entirely honest.

About

This is where visitors go to learn more about your company and what it stands for. While a timeline of the past twenty or one hundred years might be of interest to some people, the important thing to highlight is what the company is doing today. What is your mission and vision and how does it influence decisions about products, processes, and policies?

One website I browsed stated, "We are committed to the safety of employees, customers, and the environment." That company boasts on its About page that it has never experienced any chemical spills that required hazardous waste management. That seems to me like a fairly low bar. Hopefully your company has more to say about its environmental record.

Mondi has an especially extensive About section. The many subcategories, each with detailed content, indicate the scope. They include Who We Are, What We Do, Our Strategy, Our Businesses, Our Leadership, Our History, Research & Development, Certificates, Where We Operate, Corporate Contacts, and FAQs. Many of the FAQs are related to sustainability.

An About page can also include a letter or message from the CEO, updated once or twice a year or whenever there is big news to share. The letter tells stakeholders where the company stands and where its priorities lie. It's a place to talk about recent achievements, future goals, and how those relate to the health of people and the planet. A message from the CEO shows that commitments start at the top.

News/Media

When I worked as a journalist for trade magazines, the first place I often looked when researching a company was for a page labeled News, Media, or Press. That's where I could make sure I was up to date on recent announcements and press releases and download a press kit or photos to use in an article. If you want media attention on your sustainability initiatives, journalists need to be able to quickly see where you stand and what you are doing.

Press releases about new products or executive appointments do belong here. There is also an opportunity to share news related to sustainability strategy. You can publicly announce your goals and progress toward them.

One way to attract attention to your company's products or services is by writing articles in trade journals related to your industry. These are informative pieces designed to share knowledge rather than promote a solution. They can showcase your company indirectly through the byline. A news or media page can include links to any published articles.

Sustainability/ESG

Even though information about sustainability will ideally appear throughout your website, it is best to have a dedicated page. That page will likely feature a quick glance at your overall sustainability strategy and positioning, plus links to more detailed information.

There should be a link to download your latest sustainability report. If you don't have one, it's definitely time to start. The next section in this chapter talks about sustainability reporting trends and best practices.

Sustainability reports are one way to demonstrate your company's achievements. Customers may also expect certifications. They may want to see that your company has been certified to ISO 14001, a standard that requires organizations to set up an environmental management system. In some cases, customers may look for industry-specific or product-specific certifications. The sustainability or ESG page is a good place to list relevant certifications.

A sustainability page can also highlight your Code of Conduct for suppliers if you have one. You can create guidelines that are specific to your company or you can adopt a code that already exists for your industry. Chapter 4 includes some examples.

If you supply materials, parts, or tools to manufacturers, you can go through the steps of becoming a preferred supplier to your target customers. You can post any awards or certifications related to your preferred supplier status on your sustainability page. Doing so lets prospective customers know that you have met their most stringent guidelines for social and environmental responsibility.

Fuji Oil does an excellent job of providing detailed sustainability information on its website. Within the sustainability section of its website are pages devoted to sustainable procurement of palm oil, cocoa, and soybeans. The pages are impressively detailed and show the steps the company has taken to trace its supply chain back to the source.

Blog

If your company maintains a corporate blog, this is a great place to include articles that highlight your sustainability journey. You can include stories about ways that you are addressing sustainability in your products, processes, or policies. What are you doing differently, or what have you always done that has a sustainability angle?

A regular column from the CEO or other top executive shows customers that the drive for sustainability starts from the top. Again, any statements need to honestly reflect what the company is doing and not just feature buzzwords that make it look like the company is acting responsibly.

You can also invite employees to write guest blog posts about their knowledge and experiences. This gives a personal touch beyond official company news and opinion.

The blog on the website of Brewer Science is a great example. (Note: As of August 2022, the blog is embedded in the news page and does not appear on the home page menu.)

Although Brewer Science has managed a blog for many years, the focus shifted in 2021 to tell the story of the company's journey to becoming a B Corp. The blog still features educational posts related to the company's materials and applications for those products, but it mixes in more and more of the sustainability stories and posts written by employees from various departments.

Resources

Many manufacturing companies feature a Resources page where customers and prospects can go to learn more about the technologies and applications behind the company's products. Content can include application notes, product briefs, data sheets, white papers, and case studies. The last two categories are technical marketing content that can serve multiple purposes.

White papers can be a fantastic marketing tool. They educate the audience on a particular industry or technology while pointing out possible solutions to a common problem the audience may be facing. A white paper is educational and fact-based, but not impartial. The preferred solution will be something that the company offers.

The solution presented in a white paper can involve a way to reduce the consumption of energy, water, or other resources during manufacturing or over the lifetime of the product. Customers might not have thought of the environmental benefits of your company's products. A white paper is a way to point them out.

White papers do not have to be focused on a specific product as a solution. They can be about trends in an industry and how more environmentally friendly options can still meet goals for performance, cost, and time to market.

A word of caution is in order, however. The goal of honest communication applies. It is critical not to overstate or misrepresent an environmental benefit. Customers are becoming more wary, and for good reason.

Product briefs and data sheets are not obvious places to tell a sustainability story, but they can still do so. They can be revised to emphasize low energy consumption, processing temperature, or product weight if your product is ahead of competitors in these areas.

Customers who read data sheets are engineers who want to know if your product meets their technical specifications. But a more energy-saving or less toxic option will usually win out if all else is equal. If you truly offer a more environmentally friendly alternative, it is important to let people know.

On the flip side, perhaps your competitors are the ones promoting environmental benefits. In that case, it may be time to dig deeper and see if their claims hold up and how you can improve your offerings and how you market them.

Updates, Revisions, and Redesigns

As you see, there are many ways to update a website to reflect your company's sustainability journey. Whether you need minor updates, a few pages of new content, or a complete redesign depends on your starting point and what your website needs to achieve.

The design and flow of your website affects visitors' perceptions. Do links take prospective customers on a journey that allows them to discover what your company stands for and how you can help them solve their problems? Can customers quickly determine whether your products meet their expectations for features, performance, and sustainability?

I have a request: if you're redesigning your website to add new content related to your company's sustainability journey, please make it easy for visitors to find.

For example, I've been involved in judging companies for sustainability awards. Some awards allow companies to nominate themselves. If the company has submitted a form explaining why they believe they should win the award, I will start with that. Regardless, I will always look up the company's latest sustainability report.

It's frustrating when the sustainability report is hard to find. Looking over the spreadsheet that a fellow judge prepared in advance of our committee meeting, I noticed that he had said "no data" for some of the nominees. For one of them, I dug around on that company's website and found its 2021 report. That report was completed in accordance with the GRI Standards and included data on greenhouse gas emissions, waste, water use, and more. For another, I couldn't find a report either. If the organization wrote one, they sure hid it.

Sustainability Reports

Sustainability reporting has been on the rise in the past decade, which is encouraging. In 2011, only twenty percent of companies in the S&P 500 issued sustainability reports. Now that figure is over ninety percent. And smaller companies, even private companies who don't face investor pressure to report, are issuing reports.

Reporting guidelines have also gotten more stringent. In the early days of reporting, there was no consistency in which topics were included in reports. The Global Reporting Initiative updated its requirements with the GRI Standards, which went into effect in 2018. For a company to issue a report "in accordance with the GRI Standards," the report must include reporting on a long list of topics. The required topics span a range of ESG practices.

Because of the latest standards, companies cannot merely high-light areas where they are performing well and avoid mentioning areas where they fall behind. Comprehensive reporting requires measuring and including every relevant area. If you look at the whole report, it's all in there.

But stringent reporting alone doesn't guarantee in any way that companies are doing the right thing. Calculating greenhouse gas emissions is complicated, and there is no uniform practice. Companies calculate emission intensity per unit of product or revenue, which can be misleading. And it is up to each company to choose a baseline year for comparing emissions, hazardous and nonhazardous waste generation, and other measurements. Results vary depending on the baseline chosen.

Reporting, even when done according to the GRI Standards, doesn't stop companies from greenwashing. They can issue a highlights summary that emphasizes certain initiatives or new product lines while ignoring data on the rest of their products and practices. While anyone who wants to dig deeper can uncover the whole story, most people are not going to read a 100- or 200-page report cover to cover or go through financial reports in detail.

All this is not to say that reporting is useless. Far from it. It is just important to read reports and summaries with a sense of perspective and a touch of skepticism.

The more stringent reporting standards have resulted in longer reports. Some companies are responding by offering stakeholders options. They can read an executive summary with quick highlights, download the full report to see all the data, or even customize a report with the information they need to see.

Embarking on an initial sustainability report is a big undertaking best done with outside help. Software exists to guide the process by providing a framework and structure to follow. But you still need to collect the data, and an external consultant can help you see what you already have and how to find the rest. They can also ensure that it's being written in a way that will enhance knowledge and encourage action.

Even if you have issued sustainability reports for many years, it's good to keep up with best practices. Does your latest report serve the needs of your audience? Do you need to expand it or create different formats for different audience segments? It's worth asking the questions.

Certifications

A company that is truly committed to sustainability will meet, at a minimum, the most stringent global regulations related to their products and industry. They won't, for example, make their products to one standard at their factories in North America and a less stringent standard at their Asian factories.

In the discussion about sustainability and ESG website pages, I mentioned ISO 14001 certification. ISO 14001 certification demonstrates that minimum level of environmental awareness and intent. Certified companies are, at the very least, in compliance with regulations that pertain to their operations.

Chapter 4 includes a discussion of B Corp certification, which offers a higher level of commitment to ESG practices. The requirements go far beyond compliance.

Your company may have earned certifications related to particular products or to your business as a whole. Some of these are required as a license to do business in a particular location or industry. Others are optional but necessary to complete in a market. Still others will help a company stand out as being industry leading.

For companies that sell B2B, some certifications may be required to gain the business of key customers or may improve your prospects. If a manufacturer of finished goods or a retail store requires that all its suppliers use wood that is certified by the Forest Stewardship Council (FSC) or produce food that is certified organic, you have to earn those certifications if you want their business.

Certifications are useful, but they can also be confusing. It is important to decide which ones are worth pursuing. The answer depends on your industry and where you sell your products. Achieving certifications takes time and money. It needs to be done strategically.

Once you have earned certifications, you should let your customers and prospective customers know. Many certifications come with downloadable logos that you can feature on your website.

There are other ways your company can be recognized for achievements related to sustainability. When ASE Global, a leading supplier to the semiconductor industry, earned recognition on the Dow Jones Sustainability Index (DJSI) for the sixth consecutive year, they decided to publicize it.

"The DJSI listing was a huge achievement for us," ASE Global Senior Director of Corporate Marketing Communications Jennifer Yuen told me. "I started working with the team to communicate the information. We focused on improving our website presence and making the information more interesting, more available."

After reading this chapter, you probably have a good idea of how well your external communications, especially your website, showcase your sustainability strategy. If you weren't already familiar with the term greenwashing, you are now. With that awareness, you are ready to take action to improve your sustainability messaging.

Action Steps

Below are a series of six action steps you can take to help you share your sustainability journey with customers, investors, and other stakeholders. You can return to the workbook at jlfgoldstein.com/green-team as you contemplate the questions posed here.

1. Evaluate your company tag line

If your company has a tag line or slogan, how does it relate to your work? Does it inspire you, and do you believe that you and your colleagues aim to fulfill the promise behind the tag line?

2. Consider Greenwashing

Is your company guilty of greenwashing? If so, what can you do to increase transparency and shift away from misleading messaging? Greenwashing can be subtle, so this may take some work to figure out.

3. Website Audit

What does your website say about your company's values and approach to sustainability? If the information is incomplete or doesn't reflect the message you want to project, you can make a list of what you want to change.

4. Website redesign, refresh, or update

Your audit pointed the way. Now you can get to work. You might have an internal team that can make the necessary changes, or you may need to hire external designers, developers, and writers.

5. Sustainability Reporting

Action steps depend on whether you are compiling your company's first ever sustainability report or whether you have been reporting for years.

When embarking on your first annual sustainability report, it's best to set expectations for the purpose of the report. When you understand why you're writing it and share that, employees will be more willing to do their part to gather the required data.

Even companies that have been issuing reports for years can reconsider the report's purpose and make changes to make the reports more useful and relevant.

6. Certifications

Are there common certifications in your industry that your company has not earned? Are there certifications that you could pursue to stand out in your field? The topic is worth discussing.

Chapter 4

Collaboration, Not Competition

Companies that stand out for sustainability performance and sustainability communication have a few things in common. Their company culture embraces:

► Collaboration

► Openness to new ideas

► Transparency

Industry-leading companies emphasize a culture of collaboration rather than competition. That approach reflects both how they communicate inside the company and how they interact with suppliers and competitors.

As discussed in Chapter 1, more and more companies are hiring chief sustainability officers (CSOs) to lead their sustainability efforts. CSOs need to be collaborative so they can gain the trust of employees throughout the company. They need to be open to new ideas coming from departments or divisions not specifically associated with sustainability. An effective CSO will help different groups work together to make the company more environmentally responsible. The approach that we are all working toward the same goal will accelerate progress.

Healthy Competition

There can still be a place for healthy competition. Competition can be geared toward reducing waste or improving efficiency, with rewards or recognition for teams or individuals who excel. The key is that the competition is healthy. In contrast, cultures with unhealthy competition may glorify long working hours or reward productivity regardless of quality.

Companies where competition is healthy don't pit divisions or geographical locations against each other. In a collaborative culture, one team's success is a success for the whole company. Innovative ideas get shared throughout the company so that all groups and facilities can benefit.

For example, Airbus ran a challenge where they invited employees to contribute ideas in two related areas: sustainable development and inclusivity in the workplace. The company felt that these topics strongly affect the employee experience. Part of the goal of the challenge was to strengthen connections between employees and the leadership team.

Employees responded with dozens of innovative suggestions, giving the evaluation team a harder job than they expected. They needed to sift through all of the ideas and decide which ones to implement. They made sure to give feedback to everyone who submitted an idea. Culture Evolution Director Alice de Casanove told me, "I don't want to generate any frustration after this challenge, because we need to include everybody in our Innovation and Entrepreneurial journey. This challenge was a great opportunity to foster inter-site collaboration. Indeed, we were able to cross pollinate the ideas from one site to another."

In-house solutions can even be used to inspire change beyond the company's walls. Collaborative companies share their sustainability advances through media outreach, publication at industry forums, and in all their external-facing communication.

They ideally share examples not to brag but to encourage companies throughout their industry to adopt more sustainable practices. Yes, the leading companies often want to take credit for being the first to shift their processes or policies. That is fine, so long as they share in a way that allows others to join the movement.

Intel Corporation has been vocal about its sustainability actions. Its website includes a long list of awards the company has won for sustainability and responsible business practices. The company also recognizes suppliers through its Supplier Continuous Quality Improvement (SCQI) Program and annual awards. Intel relies on thousands of suppliers. By publicizing the top performers, Intel encourages companies throughout the electronics supply chain to improve in six categories, one of which is sustainability.

Leading the Way

Companies that successfully integrate sustainability throughout their organization cannot do so unless the CEO and other top executives are leading the way. The CEO and their leadership team must believe that sustainability is a top priority for the company.

Successful companies—meaning those that successfully embed sustainability into their culture—embrace the triple bottom line. They believe that people, planet, and profit are all important to the future of the business.

Both privately held and public companies can follow this approach. For public companies, investors care about share price. Financial returns still matter when companies shift their priorities toward those that improve the health and safety of employees, customers, and communities. But the notion that financial performance will suffer if sustainability takes priority does not reflect reality. When companies prioritize social and environmental goals, investors will likely benefit financially in the long run.

A 2022 study from the IBM Institute for Business Value (IBV) divides CEOs into four categories: Assessing, Complying, Operational, and Transformative.[10] The Transformative CEOs see investments in sustainability as business opportunities rather than burdensome costs.

The IBV study showed that companies with Transformational or Operational CEOs outperformed the competition. Profit margins were several percentage points higher for those companies than for companies with Assessing or Complying CEOs.

Oxford Economics and SAP surveyed 2000 executives and identified the top 9 percent as "Sustainability Leaders." These leaders set clear sustainability guidelines and communicate expectations to their workforce. Their efforts have allowed them to identify new revenue streams, reduce waste, and increase customer loyalty. Their companies are slightly more likely than those not run by Sustainability Leaders to achieve revenue growth above 10 percent.[11]

Executives commit to sustainability and demonstrate that commitment in the decisions they make. They do not make those decisions alone. The company culture is collaborative and inclusive. Every employee knows that statements of environmental responsibility are more than just words on a poster or published on the company's website. Sustainability-minded executives communicate their priorities in language that employees can understand, and employees know that the boss has their back.

Companies that stand out typically have a culture of openness. Colleagues throughout the company feel that they can speak openly about what is working and what isn't. Employees frequently share ideas and offer constructive feedback.

Sometimes idea sharing can be specific, like the example of the Fuji Oil SDG challenge from Chapter 2. Executives actively seek solutions to a particular issue they are facing from employees throughout the company.

But a true culture of openness and transparency encourages continuing, regular feedback. Employees don't need to wait until someone asks for their opinion. A project manager at an environmental consultancy told me that everyone they work with feels comfortable talking about the company's sustainability practices. This organization helps its clients improve things like energy efficiency. They want to ensure that their internal operations offer a stellar example to follow. When any employee has a concern, they bring it up to the executive team.

On the flip side, some corporate cultures encourage secrecy. These companies seem to go to extremes to be vague in communications to customers, the press, and even their employees. One division doesn't know what another one is doing. And that's often by design.

Employees in these kinds of companies may express a great allegiance to their employer, but this could be a defense mechanism. They also know that challenging authority is not accepted, and they don't want to risk losing their job. They keep any discontent to themselves and do their assigned work. The company may be very productive. It might even have a great balance sheet.

In the long run, though, cultures of secrecy are often dangerous. Employees are sometimes pressured to hide evidence of problems that affect the safety or reliability of the company's products. When employees feel that they cannot express an opinion that conflicts with the official company policy, morale is likely to suffer.

Closed cultures are also resistant to change. That means that they are likely to be left behind because the executives are not willing to rethink their business practices. They are not positioned to shift toward more environmentally sustainable policies or even to begin the conversation.

In the book *Net Positive*, the authors warn against secrecy. They emphasize the importance of openness to build trust. Shifting from a culture of secrecy to a culture of open sharing is a process that takes years. It is possible, though, and it is worth it.

Net Positive goes into the history of the Unilever Sustainable Living Plan (USLP). The company embraces the slogan, "We are Unilever" to emphasize that the entire corporation is in this together. Instead of thinking of hundreds of independent brands, the idea was to agree on principles that would guide all employees no matter where they worked.

Unilever executives understood that words matter. When they used words like "purpose" and "long term" and then acted on them, that built trust. They communicated openly about the new plan and their progress toward the goals.

As a result, the company culture shifted. It didn't happen overnight, but over many years.

This communication wasn't just to employees but also announced publicly. Once you tell the world you plan to do something, it is harder to back out.

Unilever is far from a perfect company. There are still employees who don't feel as though the lofty goals that the executives publicize filter down to their specific workplace. Public reporting that acknowledges where the company is falling short of its goals has opened it up to criticism.

Openness and transparency can be scary. Companies where employees at all levels of leadership embrace it are in a better position to respond when they are called out on a practice that doesn't match their stated goals. Instead of going on the defensive, they can ask questions and collaborate on solutions.

In *Material Value*, I tell a story about Scotts Miracle Gro. When activists attacked Scotts for causing toxic algal blooms in lakes, the company's initial reaction was to deflect blame. They quoted scientific studies showing that the source of the phosphorus that was contaminating the lakes came from elsewhere. Eventually the company shifted its approach. It admitted that its defensive stance was unhelpful, created a phosphorus-free formulation of Miracle Gro, and developed partnerships with nonprofit organizations that protect access to clean water. Those actions didn't solve the algal bloom problem, but they did increase customer trust in Scotts.

Encouraging Openness

Employees need to feel free to air concerns about the company's policies or operation without worrying about losing their job. In some companies, this type of transparent communication is encouraged. There are formal and informal channels for sharing what is going well and where there is room for improvement.

For example, Firmenich regularly surveys employees, encouraging them to "tell us how you feel" and holds frequent town hall meetings.

At some companies, employees feel the need to remain silent. They do the work required of them, keeping any concerns to themselves. They find ways to justify the cognitive dissonance between what they see as wrong with their employer or their industry and the pressure to be a loyal employee.

A culture that does not allow for any dissent is not healthy. It stifles innovation and can endanger the safety of employees and customers. The 2015 Volkswagen "dieselgate" fiasco comes to mind. As Steven Howard says in his book *Leadership Lessons from the Volkswagen Saga*, VW engaged not in accidental negligence but "deliberate corporate malfeasance." Engineers were told to do something to ensure that VW's so-called "clean diesel" cars could pass emissions tests. They proposed installing a catalytic converter that would reduce emissions, but management vetoed that idea because the part cost $385 per vehicle. The engineers were pressured to find a less expensive way to make the data look good. Their solution? Software that tricked the testing machines into reporting that toxic nitrous oxide (NOx) emissions met the standards. In reality, emissions were forty times the allowed levels.

The scandal cost VW at least $35 billion, damaged its brand reputation, and put tens of thousands of employees out of a job. VW now touts its electric vehicles. Sustainability messaging, though, is conspicuously absent from the company's website.

Before a company is willing to honestly share the good and the bad publicly, it has to develop a culture of openness inside its walls. Does your company encourage or discourage transparent communication? Here are some questions to answer in case you aren't sure.

▶ Is there a platform where you can share kudos and suggestions for improvement?

► If you observe a safety violation, how are you encouraged to report it?

► Is there a "party line" about your company that you are expected to support?

► If you have a concern about a company policy, with whom do you share it?

► Do you have an employee handbook? What does it say about airing complaints?

► Are employees encouraged to come up with new ways of doing things and to share those with colleagues?

It can be hard to take an in-depth, honest look at your company's total operations and the impact on society, both positive and negative. But unless you are willing to do so, any sustainability improvements are likely to be minor. You might be missing the biggest opportunities to change policies, processes, or products.

Addressing Cost Issues

As discussed in Chapter 2, one of the toughest bottlenecks to sustainability is cost. Companies sometimes focus on the immediate expenses associated with upgrading energy or lighting systems or buying more sustainable materials for making their products. They worry that cutting profit margins to improve sustainability will hurt the bottom line.

There can also be a sense that there are only two options when making products more environmentally friendly. One is to keep prices the same while upgrading materials or manufacturing processes. That option might shrink profit margins to such an extent that any supply chain disruption pushes them into negative territory. The company feels that it can't afford any premium for faster delivery, nor can it switch to a different supplier on short notice. Employees in charge of product design or procurement feel stuck. They can't create products that lose money.

The other option is to pass some or all of the increased expense per item to the customer. Manufacturers can follow an example set by the food industry. Organic produce costs more than conventional, but many customers choose it because they see it as a healthier option and a way to avoid pesticides.

Premium pricing only works if customers are willing to pay the higher price. If the product is promoted as more environmentally friendly, that approach might work. But many manufacturers are worried that customers will flee to competitors who offer legacy products at a lower price. This is a place where friendly competition can ease the cost barrier as more suppliers enter the market for environmentally sustainable products.

These pressures are real, but the focus on cost is often too myopic. A broader evaluation of the company's entire operating budget might disclose potential savings from more environmentally sustainable practices elsewhere. Open discussions with colleagues on the other side of the building or the other side of the world might uncover opportunities to save both money and natural resources.

For example, excess materials or parts from one division that would otherwise go to scrap might be useful to a division making a different type of product. Without company-wide collaboration, the two divisions would never discover the opportunity to save both money and resources. Multi-company and cross-industry collaborations can also yield creative uses of materials that would otherwise go to waste. Dell Computer, for example, uses reclaimed carbon fiber scrap from the aerospace industry to make laptop bases.

The above discussion assumes that more sustainable materials or packaging are more expensive per unit. That is not always the case. When product design and procurement teams investigate all the options available, they might find a more environmentally friendly alternative that costs the same or even less than what they are currently using. Perhaps the sustainability director from Chapter 2 could even find a bio-based material at a price point that wouldn't eliminate their profit.

Collaboration Across Industries

More open collaboration within a company requires a shift in perspective. It can take time for new ways of working to take hold. In general, though, once all parties can see the benefit, they are likely to agree that better collaboration helps everyone involved. They now see how improving internal communication will advance mutual sustainability goals.

The situation is trickier when it comes to collaborating across an industry. Many people are wary of sharing information with peers or competitors. They have a hard time seeing it as a situation where everyone can come out ahead. Collaboration feels especially risky. Companies don't want to reveal their weak spots because they fear that competitors will take advantage of any weakness.

There are ways to share information with less risk. It requires setting up expectation and boundaries at the outset. Initial conversations should center around mutual goals. Does everyone agree, for example, that the industry as a whole should move away from certain practices and embrace others?

As a starting point, do they agree that the world would be better off if every company in the room reduced greenhouse gas emissions? If so, then discussions can move forward. If not, then those who are not in agreement are not ready to participate. The rest can proceed without them, at least for the time being.

Companies who are ahead of the curve can lift those that have gotten a later start. Ideally, conversations can be honest and open. In reality, that is hard to do. If you set the boundaries around what information will be shared and what can be kept proprietary, that makes the situation a bit more comfortable.

There will be opportunities where multiple companies working together can have a much greater influence than individual companies working alone. Results can include reducing the cost of more environmentally friendly materials or convincing governments to develop policies that benefit companies that have committed to certain practices.

Industry associations can be helpful here, as they can host a platform for sharing resources in a non-threatening way. Some host meetings that follow the Chatham House Rule.[12] Participants are allowed to share information from the meeting but cannot identify which person or company made any particular statement. The idea is to encourage openness and honest discussion without worrying about the consequences of saying too much.

The Responsible Business Alliance (RBA) runs its annual meetings with the Chatham House Rule in place. Members of the press are not invited. I attended RBA's 2019 meeting. Participants felt free to lament lack of enforcement of laws about ethical sourcing practices. Some presenters shared slides that they wouldn't have included in a conference where the media were present and might have published their data out of context.

Becoming a B Corp

One way that companies can take a stand on ESG is to become a B Corp. B Corps are for-profit companies that are certified by B Lab., the nonprofit organization that developed the B Corp certification. These companies are, by definition, committed to the triple bottom line.

To qualify for B Corp status, companies go through a rigorous assessment process that scores them on many different aspects of ESG. They have to score high enough on the B Impact Assessment to qualify for certification. Certifications are good for three years. To renew their certification, companies must score higher than they did the last time they went through the assessment. The process automatically creates a culture of continuous improvement.

B Corp certification forces companies to examine everything they are currently doing. This is the starting point. Companies can and should celebrate that they've earned enough points to qualify.

The next question to ask is, what are we going to do so that three years from now, we've stepped up our game? It's not enough to become zero waste to landfill, or power your buildings with renewable energy, or pay your employees a living wage. It's great to do all those things. And then strive for more.

Becoming a B Corp involves all the employees at a company. Everyone can play a role in improving the score in one or more of the various ESG criteria. Achieving B Corp status also makes an organization part of a larger community where everyone is striving toward similar goals.

The first B Corps were companies that have long been associated with responsible business practices. They are known for treating the employees, customers, and the planet with respect. Seventh Generation, a brand of personal care and household cleaning products, has been certified as a B Corp since 2007, nearly a decade before it became a wholly owned subsidiary of Unilever. World Centric, a company that makes compostable food service ware, is another early B Corp. In *Material Value*, I feature an interview with Janae Lloyd of World Centric about her experience leading several B Corp re-certifications for the company.

Now, larger companies, including some in manufacturing industries, are taking the leap and pursuing B Corp certification. Several divisions of Danone earned their initial certifications in 2021 or 2022. As of 2022, over 4800 companies in seventy-nine countries have become certified. I hope that more manufacturing companies will follow their lead.

There are some caveats. Certification is no guarantee that a company is doing everything it can to be environmentally sustainable. Some B Corps have been criticized for lacking in certain areas or overstating their environmental credentials. Companies need a minimum score to become certified, but there are many ways to attain that. Depending on their industry, they might emphasize the community or employee welfare aspects of ESG.

The B Corp certification says a lot about a company's approach to business. But this is just one possible path. Many companies do not want to go through the assessment and certification process. That's understandable because it is a major undertaking. Only a small percentage of the companies that apply each year gain each enough points to qualify for certification. Companies that do not wish to go through the process or have not yet qualified can still choose suppliers that are certified as B Corps. They can also use the B Corp assessment tool as an informal way to get insight into where they are doing well and where they are lacking.

Industry Associations

There are many forward-thinking professionals in multiple industries who want to do more to advance sustainability at their company. They are actively searching for tools and resources that will help their company improve.

The Conference Board is one helpful resource. It is a nonprofit organization that has been around for over 100 years supporting CEOs concerned about creating safe, healthy workplaces. Today, it comprises several centers focused on specific aspects of business:

- ► Economic Development
- ► Economy, Strategy, and Finance
- ► Environmental, Social, and Governance
- ► Human Capital
- ► Marketing and Communications

All of these aspects are related to one another. The Conference Board offers resources to help companies face many factors that affect the business world, from supply chain disruption to social and political upheaval. ESG is definitely a growing issue.

While The Conference Board serves executives in many different industries, associations are often industry-specific. They serve as a resource for member companies. They can also be a platform for promoting the industry and its products. An association representing hundreds of businesses has more influence than individual companies acting alone. This is especially true for industries made up of small businesses.

The role of industry associations is to support their members. They have the opportunity to promote more sustainable and just business practices. That doesn't mean, however, that they necessarily do so. In some cases, industry associations lobby against environmental regulations that they feel would cost their members money.

Associations often justify practices and policies that benefit their industry. That response is natural. The problem is when associations prioritize short-term profits of their members over social and environmental responsibility.

In my research, I spoke to professionals at several associations to find out what they are hearing from their members and what changes they would like to see in their industry.

In some cases, member companies are not aware of the role their business or their industry can play in advancing (or stifling) sustainability. BIFMA, the Business and Institutional Furniture Manufacturers Association, is one example. Member companies make furniture that meets association and industry standards for safety and performance. They see safety and performance as important, but there's a gap in awareness when it comes to sustainability. Steve Kooy, Technical Director of Health and Sustainability at BIFMA, said, "I'd definitely like to get more people to understand the value we bring, but also from a sustainability perspective, what our industry or even what their individual company is doing. I think, honestly, people don't realize how much good is going on in the world."

Up and Down the Supply Chain

Individual companies cannot reach their sustainability goals independently. While they can make progress by changing processes and policies inside their walls, systemic change requires them to reach out up and down the supply chain.

Greenhouse gas emissions, for example, are divided into three scopes. Scope 1 includes emissions from a company's operations. Scope 2 encompasses energy use to power company-owned buildings. Scope 3 extends to the entire supply chain, from procurement of materials through use and eventual disposal of the end product.

Scope 1 and 2 emissions are the easiest to control and reduce. But Scope 3 emissions are often the largest contributor to overall greenhouse gas emissions. That means that companies need to understand them and report on them. Doing so requires talking with suppliers and customers.

Suppliers are also key to reducing waste and water consumption. The choice of supplier can help or hinder progress toward reduction goals.

Many original equipment manufacturers (OEMs) expect all their suppliers to meet certain standards for social and environmental responsibility. They set minimum guidelines required to earn their business. In some cases, they have different tiers or award their top suppliers with special recognition.

The Responsible Business Alliance (RBA) is a coalition of hundreds of companies in the electronics industry. Members must agree to the RBA Code of Conduct. The Code outlines expectations that member companies agree to uphold. The code includes sections on labor practices, employee health and safety, environmental responsibility, business ethics, and management systems.

The Code considers compliance with global and local laws and regulations as a bare minimum. Participants also need to implement plans to manage energy consumption, water use, and waste handling. They need to disclose information about business practices.

Transparent communication is one of the aspects of the required management system. As the Code states, the system should include "A process for communicating clear and accurate information about [the] participant's policies, practices, expectations, and performance to workers, suppliers, and customers."

Because suppliers to RBA member companies must also agree to the RBA Code of Conduct, RBA's reach extends far beyond its membership. The RBA website[13] estimates that those suppliers represent 3.5 million workers in over 120 countries.

The RBA is just one example of an organization that expects its members to follow a set of environmental standards. Similar organizations exist for many industries. Companies that want to become more sustainable will likely benefit by getting involved. Membership can build credibility, open up business opportunities, and give you a better sense of the direction your industry is headed.

Goal Setting

A sustainability agenda involves setting goals. For example, a company commits to net zero carbon by 2050 or, better yet, by 2040 or 2030. It sets shorter term goals that are one, two, or five years out to encourage and celebrate progress along the way. There are additional goals for waste reduction and water management. Social initiatives involving worker health and safety are likely incorporated.

Goals are important and necessary. Merely setting them, however, is not enough. Companies need concrete plans to achieve those goals. People have told me that their company has a goal to reduce greenhouse gas emissions by a certain percentage. They sometimes also say they have no idea how the company will accomplish this goal. It seems out of reach and they are uncertain about what steps are necessary to get there.

Employees may feel powerless. If the end point feels too distant, they don't believe they can do anything to move toward it. So, they continue business as usual and ignore the looming disaster.

Clear communication alone won't solve the problem. At the same time, without it, progress cannot happen. Employees throughout the company need to understand the goals and be able to relate them to their work. When everyone sees how they can be part of the solution, they will feel empowered to make a difference. Sustainability standards or certification processes offer guidance on ways to involve all employees in making the workplace more sustainable.

Environmental challenges like the example from Airbus in this chapter are one way to spur innovation and employee engagement. These will likely be most successful when employees understand the context. It needs to be more than a one-time program. Instead, a challenge can help launch an environment where employees believe that management will listen to their ideas. More than just listening, the leaders will engage in discussions about which ideas are feasible and which ones aren't and why.

Industry standards organizations also address sustainability. SEMI, which represents the electronics manufacturing and design supply chain, has been developing technology roadmaps for decades. Representatives from member companies contribute their ideas and ensure that the roadmaps are relevant. Now SEMI is developing its first sustainability roadmap. The organization is encouraging member companies to join the Sustainability Advisory Council and demonstrate that the industry is committed to collaboration when it comes to setting a standard.

When Your Workplace is Not Supportive

The beginning of this chapter talked about the benefits of a collaborative and open culture in promoting sustainability. On the flip side, a culture of stiff competition and secrecy makes progress difficult.

Employees who find themselves working at a company where openness is not encouraged have several options:

1. **Ignore your misgivings.** Do your assigned work and decide that keeping your current job is the highest priority. This can feel like the easy way out, but if you care deeply about people and the environment, your work will likely cause you emotional stress. That may not be "sustainable" in the long run.

2. **Speak up and share your concerns.** This does not mean standing up at an all-hands meeting and telling the executives how you think the company culture ought to change. Instead, it is best to start the conversation with one trusted colleague. Perhaps you can start a grass roots shift.

A small group speaking up is more effective than a single individual to start things moving. If one person makes waves, their boss can show them the door. It is different if several employees or an entire group approaches their supervisor with concrete suggestions. Management probably cannot afford to fire all of you.

3. **Leave your job for another at a company where the culture is a better fit for your values.** True, you won't do anything to change the situation at your current employer. But in a more open culture, you can feel part of an organization where sustainability is a priority. And you can do more to offer solutions.

Switching jobs is not without risks, especially if you leave before you have secured a new position. But if the risk to your mental health is greater if you stay where you are and you aren't willing or able to make the effort to instigate change there, it might be the best option.

This chapter has emphasized the importance of openness and collaboration. Collaboration applies both within an organization and outside it. Suppliers and industry associations are important resources for achieving your sustainability goals and joining a community of like-minded companies is a great way to propel your company forward.

Action Steps

Below are some topics to contemplate as you consider your company's culture and opportunities for collaboration. If you have not yet downloaded the workbook at jlfgoldstein.com/green-team, now would be a fine time to do that.

1. Corporate culture review

You considered your company's mission and vision in Chapter 2. This question is related but a bit different. Where does your company culture lie on the spectrum from competitive to collaborative? Has it evolved over time or been the same for decades? The answers will give you clues about how likely it is that your culture will shift toward a more collaborative one.

2. Communicating your sustainability goals

What does your sustainability pathway look like over the next two, five, ten, or twenty years? Are your goals ambitious enough in the long term while still giving you the chance to see success in small steps? Have you shared your goals with employees in terms they can understand and given them the tools to contribute to reaching the goals? What are you saying publicly about your sustainability goals?

3. Your supply chain

Your reach extends up and down your supply chain. How are you communicating your company's sustainability goals to suppliers and customers? How are you engaging them in helping you reach goals that benefit all parties? You can look for opportunities to build connections that will help not only your company but your entire industry.

4. Other partnerships

Look for opportunities to join industry associations. Where can you contribute your expertise toward advancing sustainability for the entire industry? Where can you join the conversation to learn from others?

Chapter 5

Put It All Together

Many companies struggle to figure out how to best share their sustainability message in a way that resonates. The last three chapters offered insight into how to approach internal and external communication and the benefits of embracing a collaborative company culture. Now it is time to tie it all together and come up with a more comprehensive plan.

Sharing Your Message

In 2021, I attended a webinar about this topic from The Conference Board. The presenters echoed my experience when they said they are hearing the same concerns from hundreds of business leaders, investors, and regulators. People want to know how to tell a story that is true to the business culture. They worry about how to make the story consistent when talking to multiple audiences. On this topic, Calvin Cheng, Global Materials Director of Procter & Gamble (P&G), said, "I think the most challenging part is trying to find a way to drive consensus on what sustainability means for the company, and then also finding a holistic, sustainable message to give to all of our consumers."

Finding one consistent message is indeed a daunting challenge for a multinational corporation like P&G with hundreds of brands and multiple, somewhat independent, business units. Smaller companies struggle with similar issues. Their products might not cover as broad a spectrum, but they still need to tailor messaging to multiple customer groups. For example, a company that makes sensors for consumer electronics, medical devices, and automotive applications will design and promote its products differently for each market. There are, however, overlaps in the technology. Might the company find a universal sustainability message that reflects the company's values and its customers' needs?

When considering the issues above, it is best to understand your starting point.

- ▶ Where does your company stand on sustainability?

- ▶ How are you talking about it?

- ▶ Do your words and actions match?

Next, envision your goals. This exercise can build on the reflections from Chapter 2 about mission, vision, and values.

- ▶ What kind of company do you want to become?

- ▶ How do you want to show up in the world?

- ▶ How do you want to treat your employees, your customers, and all stakeholders?

You might see the types of mismatches that my clients sometimes express between how their company is currently approaching sustainability and how they wish things could evolve. Once you recognize gaps, you can then explore ways to bridge them. You may find resources inside or outside your company—people, revenue streams, and technology—that can help fill the gaps.

The actions your company will be ready to take depends on your starting point. In *Making Sustainability Work,* authors Marc Epstein and Adriana Rejc Buhovac outline three stages that companies go through in developing a sustainability strategy.

Stage 1 is where companies realize that they need to be more environmentally sustainable. They begin adopting policies that will bring them into compliance with environmental regulations in the countries and cities where they operate. The risks of penalties are often what has motivated them to start the journey. They want to avoid fees for non-compliance and don't want to lose customers.

At stage 2, companies see that they can move beyond compliance and gain a competitive advantage if they improve their sustainability programs. They are looking more deeply into their entire operations to find opportunities to improve safety, save natural resources, and reduce energy use. They see that these actions can improve the quality of their products and their reputation as a responsible company.

The final stage is where companies integrate ESG issues throughout their organization. Corporate practices and policies make sustainability a top priority. Such policies extend to all divisions and all geographical locations. Stage 3 companies are engaged in proactive planning to meet stringent one-year, five-year, and ten-year goals.

It is encouraging to see more companies realizing the importance of a comprehensive sustainability strategy. That strategy will have the greatest chance of success if employees and customers are aware of it and understand what it has to do with them. Consistent, clear messaging will help.

The Five Stages of Sustainability Communications Revisited

Your company's sustainability communication journey parallels its overall sustainability journey. I divide the sustainability communication path into five distinct stages that break down a company's evolution from unaware to fully engaged. I mentioned these stages briefly in Chapter 1.

To clarify, these stages are separate from the three stages proposed in *Making Sustainability Work*. From here on out, all reference to stages of a company's journey refer to my Five Stages of Sustainability Communications. These stages show the maturity of both sustainability programs and how companies communicate their values and actions.

Stage 1: Unaware

At this point, sustainability is not something that ever comes up at work. It is not a topic for department updates and doesn't appear on the agenda at board meetings or executive briefings. There are no internal sustainability programs.

The company website says nothing about sustainability. There is no sustainability or CSR page and no reporting.

Individual employees probably care, and some might even be striving toward being more environmentally responsible at home. They are trying to drive less, recycle more, and buy less stuff. But they don't connect a green lifestyle to what they do at work.

Many companies are still at this stage even in 2022. They are, for the most part, small businesses. They serve industries that haven't seen much public or customer pressure to incorporate sustainability into their operations.

Stage 2: Vaguely Aware

This stage is where informal discussions are starting. Executives have woken up to the idea that sustainability can be relevant to their company. They are likely responding to what they have heard in the news or murmurings from employees or customers.

The website might have generic or vague statements about sustainability, but they are done without any serious thought. There is no strategy behind the content.

This stage is similar to an early stage in the overall sustainability journey where a company starts by merely complying with local environmental regulations instead of ignoring them and paying a fee.

Stage 3: Aware

This is a midpoint where awareness has built to the point where top management realizes that they need to do something to address sustainability. They are developing a plan and considering setting goals. They may have assigned a director-level employee or VP to be in charge of building a sustainability agenda.

Employees are getting the message that sustainability is on the company agenda. They know how to find the company's sustainability report if they want to read it. Depending on their role, though, they might or might not think that the sustainability journey involves them personally.

One risk at this stage is that the company jumps onto the sustainability bandwagon without thoroughly considering how to integrate sustainability into the company culture. They might task the marketing department with updating external communications too soon.

Stage 4: Involved

Companies at this stage have done a lot of the work outlined in Chapters 2 and 3 of this book. They have committed to sustainability goals and have communicated the goals to employees. They have an effective sustainability leader who has the support of the CEO.

Sustainability and marketing professionals have a good working relationship and feel that they are moving forward together. Sustainability reporting has become more ingrained, and the company is actively working to improve on gaps that the data has revealed. The sustainability or ESG page on the website is detailed and reflects the company's values. Sustainability-related content is continually added.

There are still opportunities for improvement. The executives understand how the company's purpose is connected to sustainability, but the message might not be clear to all employees. Some departments or divisions might be lagging because they aren't as connected to the corporate sustainability group as they could be.

Stage 5: Fully Engaged

Companies at stage 5 are industry leaders, both in acting on sustainability and communicating about it within and outside their organization. A stage 5 company has a mission and vision that proclaims a desire to make the world a better place because of its products and services. The mission and vision are not merely inspiring words on the company's website and on its walls but are ingrained into decision-making at all levels.

Employees are informed and empowered. In every division and every geographical location, they know where their employer stands on sustainability. They understand what the mission and vision mean and are proud to work at a company that values their contributions and is working toward a greater purpose than just making money. They know that if they suggest a new idea or policy change, management will listen. Even if the company doesn't implement their suggestion, they feel heard and encouraged to keep thinking creatively.

External communications, whether directed at customers, suppliers, or investors, is aligned with the company's purpose and mission. Messaging is consistent and aligns with what is happening inside the company's walls. Website visitors can easily find information about the company's sustainability goals and progress toward those goals. The marketing team is aware of the risks of greenwashing and reviews all content to ensure that it is not overselling environmental claims.

Stage 5 companies may be certified as B Corps, but they do not have to be. As mentioned in Chapter 4, B Corp certification is only one path toward becoming a more responsible and sustainable business. Not all B Corps are at stage 5, but they aspire to get there. The continuous improvement model required for recertification will help them progress.

Readiness to Act

Now that you understand the five stages, let's look at how they relate to a company's readiness to act on sustainability. Companies at stage 1 are not yet ready to respond to external pressures. Their executives are unlikely to read a book like this one or the many excellent books I recommend. That is unfortunate, because they are likely to continue business as usual until they can no longer do so. At that point, it might be too late.

At the other end of the spectrum, stage 5 companies are the examples that others look to as inspiration. They have earned the trust of their customers and suppliers. They have the leverage to lift all their suppliers and work with their competitors to improve sustainability throughout their industry.

Industry leaders also recognize that they are in the public eye. As such, any missteps get magnified. Executives understand the importance of keeping communication lines open to maintain trust.

Companies in stages 2 through 4 are ready and willing to make progress. They have embarked on a journey that can lead to honest, transparent communication about sustainability throughout their company and to the outside world. Still, they face many potential bottlenecks. The path isn't necessarily clear.

Even companies that are well aware of the problem of greenwashing are doing it. They don't necessarily intend to mislead customers or the public. Their leaders want to do and say the right thing, but it isn't easy.

Just because leaders at mid-stage companies can see examples of companies who are a stage or two ahead of them doesn't mean that they know how to get there. They can benefit from an external facilitator or consultant who can help them identify bottlenecks and move to the next stage. Consultants can look at their operations as both an objective observer and as an expert with knowledge and insights to share.

Where does your company stand along the Five Stages of Sustainability Communications? If you aren't sure, I offer comprehensive assessments where I talk to you and your colleagues and audit your website. At the end, you will receive a report showing your current stage and suggestions for the next steps.

Do you want to keep progressing until you reach stage 5? If so, I congratulate you on your intention. Now it is time to implement a framework that will help you reach your goals. I offer one way to go about that with a systematic approach.

The C3 Framework

I've developed a framework that guides companies through the Five Stages of Sustainability Communications. It consists of three pillars, and I call it C3. The pillars are, in order:

I. Connection

II. Communication

III. Content

You can see an outline of the program and the benefits to participants at *https://jlfgoldstein.com/c3-sustainability*. Here are the main points for each pillar.

Connection

The first pillar builds on the information presented in Chapter 2 about internal communication. Connection is about getting the right people in the room and building trust. That starts with building a functional sustainability team within the organization. It often involves outside collaboration via participation in industry groups, creating a sustainability advisory board, or hiring consultants to help create the necessary connections between employees.

When you have an effective team, you can work together to determine the top priorities to address immediately to improve sustainability performance. You can create an environment where everyone feels that they are working toward a common goal.

Steve Kooy, the furniture manufacturers' association leader I introduced in Chapter 4, makes an important point. "You can't start fourteen new initiatives midstream and expect good results," he told me. "At the same time, both from a personal standpoint and certainly a communication and publicity standpoint, you can't say, oh, that doesn't matter … I think it's just getting everyone in the room to say, can we agree on the top three?"

Building connections inside the company is one way to avoid the problem Steve alludes to where everyone is racing off in a different direction with possibly conflicting agendas. A key connection point is the one between sustainability and marketing groups. You can evaluate whether and how those teams interact with each other. If they are invested in improving their connection, the first module of the C3 program can lead them in the right direction.

If the sustainability and marketing groups aren't even talking to one another, the first goal might be to open up a dialog. If the two departments interact but distrust each other, the next step is to build trust. That will probably require a facilitator or coach.

There are many other opportunities to build connections within and outside an organization. Connections can involve collaboration with peers (competitors), suppliers, customers, and financial institutions. The stronger the connections, the more power you will have to progress on sustainability goals.

Communication

Communication is the central pillar. It combines concepts from Chapters 2, 3, and 4. Without clear, honest communication, merely forming a team and creating content will not get you the results you want.

As I stated in the Introduction to this book, what you say within and beyond your walls affects your ability to attract and retain employees, customers, and investors. Communication builds on connection. It is about nurturing those connections.

Open communication helps break through resistance to spending time and money on sustainability programs. When leaders show that they are listening and understand what different individuals or groups need, that's when creative ideas can move forward. The examples in Chapter 4 demonstrate the value of an environment where employees can share what is going well and where they see problems.

Open communication with customers is also critical. They don't need to know all the details about what goes on inside your company, but they need honest answers to their questions. They want to make an informed decision about whether to do business with you.

It can be challenging to determine what to say when. Part of the communication piece involves honest discussion inside the company about greenwashing. You might be doing it without realizing it. Or, in an effort to avoid overselling your sustainability progress, you might not be telling a strong enough story about what you have already accomplished.

If you listen to your customers, they will guide you. They will tell you, either directly or indirectly, what's working and what isn't. What are people writing in product reviews? What are they buying? What are customers in your industry saying they want?

The advice of listening to customers may seem obvious, but many companies don't do it early enough. If you wait until the media is shouting about some harm your company or industry is causing, you will be scrambling to catch up and make changes.

Content

Content, the primary focus of Chapter 3, is the last pillar for an important reason. Only once you have strengthened connections and improved communication is it time to revisit your external-facing content. What messages are you sending, and are they consistent with the company's values and sustainability strategy?

You are probably constantly creating new content in the form of internal updates, news announcements, sales copy for new products, website updates, quarterly or annual reports, and more. The concept of the content pillar is to pause and re-evaluate your content creation with a sustainability lens. The self-reflection and mindset shift from the first two pillars inform marketing teams how to approach content creation.

The story you tell yourselves inside your company about sustainability should first spread throughout the organization. What content are you sharing with employees, and who is creating it? Do employees from various departments have the chance to contribute if they want to do that?

The next step is to ensure that content directed at customers and investors is aligned with your mission, vision, and purpose. That evaluation encompasses all of ESG—environmental, social, and governance factors. People are listening more critically than ever.

There is always an opportunity to revise what you are telling your various stakeholders. At the same time, if your messaging keeps shifting, that will not build trust. That is why pausing to reflect and choose a content strategy is important.

Another aspect of externally facing content is choosing who will create it. Will you rely on in-house writers or hire an agency or freelancers? Any of these options can be successful. The best choice will depend on the size of your marketing team and their skills, the level of industry and technical knowledge you require in your messaging, and your budget. You can, of course, choose a blend of in-house and outsourced writers.

Where to Start

As mentioned earlier in this chapter, the actions your company needs to take depend on your starting point. You can return to the action steps sections of previous chapters for guidance. To make this easier, I've put all the discussion questions into a workbook so you can see it all in one place. You can download the workbook at *jlfgoldstein.com/green-team*.

Overall, as you review the content of this book, you may consider one of several approaches:

- ▶ Share the book with your colleagues so that you can jointly develop a plan to implement the relevant suggestions.

- ▶ Hold a company retreat for department and division leaders where you address sustainability communications and decide how you want to move forward.

► Bring in one or more external consultants to train a group of employees on the topics. Depending on your needs, these could be consultants specializing in sustainability, change management, or team building.

► Send the employee in charge of sustainability to an external training program so they can bring their learning back to their team. That person might be the CSO, Sustainability Director, or VP of another department.

One option for training is to enroll in my C3 program. I invite you to read the details at *jlfgoldstein.com/c3-sustainability* and book a call with me to discuss your needs and how the program can best help you achieve your goals. The general framework can be adapted to work for a cohort of sustainability directors from multiple companies or department heads from one company. Both approaches have advantages and limitations.

With a mixed group, participants get insight into what other companies are doing. They can learn from each other. One company might share a story about a program and another company can adapt it to their needs. Participants can also benefit from learning that they are not alone. Others in different businesses and different industries share the same concerns. Group discussions can lead to new insights, especially with a facilitator that directs the conversation toward brainstorming solutions.

One limitation of a mixed group is that participants might not feel comfortable sharing what is going on inside the company. They might hold back on details because they don't want to make their company look bad. Even though the goal is honest communication, it can be hard to be completely open in front of peers from outside your company. When the program participants are all from the same company, that overcomes one barrier to honest sharing. Discussions can dig deeper into the reasons behind the obstacles. Also, when an entire team undergoes training together, they all gain knowledge they can implement immediately without needing to bring colleagues up to speed.

That said, a more diverse group sometimes leads to more creative solutions. Cross-industry collaboration is beneficial. The trick is setting up the right group of people to encourage productive interaction. Before enrolling a cohort from multiple organizations, I will talk to everyone first to build a group that will be most likely to work well together.

As you decide where to go from here, the key is to choose a path that will help you reach your sustainability goals while nurturing a supportive, collaborative atmosphere in your workplace. When your company embraces sustainability as a key priority, the culture will shift in a positive direction. Open, honest communication will not solve all the challenges you will face in making your products and your supply chain more sustainable. But without those strong connections inside your company and beyond its walls, progress will be so much harder.

Action Steps

I hope that this book has given you some ideas of what your next steps should be. Chapters 1 through 4 concluded with action steps. Here, I leave you with three suggestions.

1. Review the action steps from the previous chapters. If you are using the workbook, now is the perfect time to return to any that you skipped over.

2. Determine where in the five stages of sustainability communications your company falls. If you aren't sure, you might benefit from an assessment. You can find the details at jlfgoldstein.com/services.

3. Commit to a plan that will help you progress to the next stage.

If this book has given you the tools you need to advance sustainability communications at your company, I am delighted. Please reach out and share your success. If you feel that you need more support, please reach out also. Let's talk about how I can help. I am on a mission to make manufacturing more environmentally responsible, and I can't do it alone. Thanks for your interest in learning and taking your company to the next level so you can be part of the solution. Good luck!

Letter to Readers

Thank you for picking up this book and reading it. If you found it useful, many people in your circle probably will as well. Please help spread the word by posting an online review and mentioning the book on social media.

If you have not already downloaded the free workbook with all the action steps questions, please do so at *jlfgoldstein.com/green-team*.

You may be interested in the programs I offer to manufacturing companies:

► *Five Stages of Sustainability Communications Assessment.* An online quiz, conversations with employees, and a website audit will tell you where your company lands. See *jlfgoldstein.com/ services*.

► *C3 Program.* This interactive 12-week program offers expert guidance and practical support so you can build your sustainability communications strategy and better integrate sustainability into your company's culture. See *jlfgoldstein.com/C3-sustainability*.

Have you read my previous books? You can find *Material Value* and *Rethink the Bins* at *juliagoldsteinauthor.com* and everywhere books are sold.

I appreciate my readers. Thanks again for your support,

Julia

Acknowledgments

This book started with a series of interviews I conducted to learn more about the challenges facing sustainability professionals, especially those new to the role. My original plan was to write a short report on my findings to distribute to everyone I interviewed. As I started writing, I realized that I could reach more people if I expanded it into a book.

I appreciate everyone who took the time to share their stories with me. To Scott Breen, Calvin Cheng, Alice de Casanove, Bruce Kim, Steve Kooy, and Jennifer Yuen: thank you for permission to quote you in this manuscript. To everyone else who appears anonymously and those I didn't quote directly: your words also helped shape this book.

After I completed the first draft of this manuscript, I happened to discover Carla King's writing critique course through the Nonfiction Authors Association. I am glad that the timing worked out and I was able to receive excellent feedback from group members. Thanks, Paula Bird, Patty Brodgon, John Daniewicz, Margot Kelman, Judy Reyes, Kenneth Robinson, Odile Sullivan-Tarazi, Lisa Thee, Mark Sharp, and Stacia Yoon for your insightful suggestions.

I want to thank my business coaches Jay Allyson Dempster and Renée Blasky for your encouragement and support, both for writing this book and for developing my consulting programs. You believe that my work deserves to be out in the world and have urged me to share my knowledge and how I can help manufacturing businesses.

Thanks to the team of editing and design professionals who transformed this book from a semi-polished manuscript to a finished book. The key to producing a book that belongs on the shelves and the online retail sites alongside those from major publishing houses is to hire people with the right expertise. Thanks in advance to everyone who posts a glowing review, shares this book with friends and colleagues, and lets more people know that it exists.

About the Author

Author photograph © Dan Devries

Julia Goldstein is an author and business owner on a mission to make manufacturing more environmentally responsible. She has a background in engineering, journalism, content writing, and teaching and holds a PhD in materials science. Julia's company, *JLFG Communications*, works with manufacturers to help them connect business goals, environmental action, and effective communication strategies. JLFG Communications is a proud member of the American Sustainable Business Network and One Percent for the Planet.

Julia's first book, *Material Value: More Sustainable, Less Wasteful Manufacturing of Everything from Cell Phones to Cleaning Products*, is a B.R.A.G Medallion Honoree, Finalist in the 2019 San Francisco Writers Contest, and Semifinalist for the 2020 Nonfiction BookLife Prize. She is also the author of *Rethink the Bins: Your Guide to Smart Recycling and Less Household Waste*, which received a Gold award from the Nonfiction Authors Association.

Julia lives in the beautiful Pacific Northwest where she enjoys a view of trees out the window of her home office. She appreciates getting outdoors every day and loves running, hiking, bicycling, and open water swimming.

You can learn more about Julia and join her online community at *jlfgoldstein.com* and *juliagoldsteinauthor.com*.

Resources

List of Acronyms

B2B—Business to business

B2C—Business to consumer

BIFMA—The Business and Institutional Furniture Manufacturers Association

CEO—Chief Executive Officer

CSO—Chief Sustainability Officer

CSR—Corporate social responsibility

DJSI—Dow Jones Sustainability Index

ESG—Environmental, social, and governance

GRI—Global Reporting Initiative

IBV—IBM Institute for Business Value

ISO—International Standards Organization

LCA—Life cycle analysis

NOx—Nitrous oxide

OEM—Original equipment manufacturer

RBA—Responsible Business Alliance

RMI—Responsible Minerals Alliance

SDG—Sustainable Development Goals

USLP—Unilever Sustainable Living Plan

Recommended Books

Attenborough, David, and Jonnie Hughes. *Life on Our Planet: My Witness Statement and a Vision for the Future.* New York: Hachette Book Group, 2020.

Bilott, Robert, and Tom Shroder. *Exposure: Poisoned Water, Corporate Greed and One Lawyer's Twenty-Year Battle against DuPont.* London: Simon & Schuster, 2020.

Epstein, Marc J, and Adriana Rejc Buhovac. *Making Sustainability Work: Best Practices in Managing and Measuring Corporate Social, Environmental, and Economic Impacts.* Second edition. San Francisco: Berrett-Koehler Publishers, 2014.

Goldstein, Julia L F. *Material Value: More Sustainable, Less Wasteful Manufacturing of Everything from Cell Phones to Cleaning Products.* Redmond, WA: Bebo Press, 2019.

———*Rethink the Bins: Your Guide to Smart Recycling and Less Household Waste.* Redmond, WA: Bebo Press, 2020.

Howard, Steven B. *Leadership Lessons from the Volkswagen Saga.* Palm Springs, CA: Caliente Press, 2017.

Polman, Paul, and Andrew S Winston. *Net Positive: How Courageous Companies Thrive by Giving More than They Take.* Boston, Ma: Harvard Business Review Press, 2021.

Raworth, Kate. *Doughnut Economics: Seven Ways to Think like a 21st-Century Economist.* London: Random House Business Books, 2017.

Notes

1 Ernst & Young, "ESG disclosures take center stage as investors raise stakes to assess company performance," *https://www.ey.com/en_gl/news/2020/07/esg-disclosures-take-center-stage-as-investors-raise-stakes-to-assess-company-performance*. Accessed June 18, 2022.

2 The Economist Intelligence Unit, "An Eco-wakening: Measuring global awareness, engagement and action for nature," May 2021, *https://www.worldwildlife.org/publications/an-eco-wakening-measuring-awareness-engagement-and-action-for-nature*. Accessed June 18, 2022.

3 Cain, Áine, "Walmart Employees Dish on What It's Actually like to Work at the Retail Giant." *Business Insider.* August 2, 2018. *https://www.businessinsider.com/walmart-store-employees-describe-working-retail-giant-2018-7#the-company-donates-more-money-than-you-might-think-8*. Accessed June 27, 2022.

4 Goldstein, Julia, "Sustainability 101: Earth Day and Eco-Design," *https://www.3dincites.com/2022/04/sustainability-101-earth-day-and-eco-design/*

5 United States Environmental Protection Agency, "Sources of Greenhouse Gas Emissions," *https://www.epa.gov/ghgemissions/sources-greenhouse-gas-emissions*. Accessed June 14, 2022.

6 Symrise AG. 2021. "The Power of Holistic Action: Corporate Report 2020." Symrise.com. March 9, 2021. *https://www.symrise.com/sustainability/reports-policies-standards-audits/#our-corporate-reports*.

7 "CDP Homepage." n.d. *www.cdp.net*. Accessed June 27, 2022.

8 "GRI - Sector Program." n.d. *www.globalreporting.org*. Accessed June 27, 2022. *https://www.globalreporting.org/standards/sector-program*.

9 "LEARN." n.d. Clean Creatives. *https://cleancreatives.org/learn*

10 IBM Institute for Business Value. 2022. "CEO Study: Own Your Impact." IBM. May 2022. *https://www.ibm.com/thought-leadership/institute-business-value/en-us/c-suite-study/ceo*.

11 SAP. 2022. "Oxford Economics and SAP Study: Gap to Going Green | SAP News." SAP News Center. June 5, 2022. *https://news.sap.com/2022/06/oxford-economics-and-sap-study-gap-going-green/*.

12 "Chatham House Rule." n.d. Chatham House – International Affairs Think Tank. *https://www.chathamhouse.org/about-us/chatham-house-rule*

13 "About the RBA." n.d. *www.responsiblebusiness.org*. *https://www.responsiblebusiness.org/about/rba/*

Made in United States
North Haven, CT
25 April 2023

35859456R00076